Bible
Answers

Abridged from
Bible Readings for the Home

REVIEW AND HERALD® PUBLISHING ASSOCIATION

Since 1861 | www.reviewandherald.com

Fourth edition
Copyright © 1914, 1935, 1943, 1949, 1957, 1962, 1989, 2012,
Review and Herald® Publishing Association
International copyright secured

Cover design by Bryan Gray / Review and Herald® Design
Interior designed by Emily Ford / Review and Herald® Design
Typeset: 11/13 Minion Pro

Interior Illustrations:
 pp. 4 © Steve Creitz
 pp. 10, 42, 98, © Nathan Greene / nathangreenestudio.com
 pp. 27, 28, 54, 56, © Lars Justinen/goodsalt.com
 All other illustrations © Review and Herald Publishing Association

PRINTED IN U.S.A.

16 15 14 13 12   5 4 3 2 1

R&H Cataloging Service
Bible answers: abridged from Bible readings for the home

1. Bible—Study and teaching.

220.7

ISBN 978-0-8280-2685-7

Contents

The Good News About

Chapter 1: **The Future** 5

Chapter 2: **The Bible** 7

Chapter 3: **God** 12

Chapter 4: **The End of Sin and Suffering** 14

Chapter 5: **The Man Who Was God** 17

Chapter 6: **Our Future Home** 19

Chapter 7: **Salvation** 25

Chapter 8: **Living for Christ** 29

Chapter 9: **The End of the World** 31

Chapter 10: **The Coming King** 36

Chapter 11: **The Creator** 40

Chapter 12: **God's Unchangeable Day** 48

Chapter 13: **God's Everlasting Grace** 52

Chapter 14: **Baptism** 54

Chapter 15: **Death** 57

Chapter 16: **Hell** 62

Chapter 17: **A Thousand Years of Peace** 64

Chapter 18: **The Judgment** 67

Chapter 19: **Growth in Christ** 75

Chapter 20: **God's People** 81

Chapter 21: **Financial Security** 90

Chapter 22: **Vibrant Health** 92

Chapter 23: **The Comforter** 96

Chapter 24: **Following Christ** 104

Index 110

Chapter 1

The Good News About
The Future

The King's Dream

What statement did Nebuchadnezzar, king of Babylon, make to his wise men whom he had assembled?

"And the king said to them, *'I have had a dream, and my spirit is anxious to know the dream.'*" Daniel 2:3.

After being threatened with death if they did not make known the dream and the interpretation, what did the wise men say to the king?

"The Chaldeans answered the king, and said, *'There is not a man on earth who can tell the king's matter;* therefore no king, lord, or ruler has ever asked such things of any magician, astrologer, or Chaldean. It is a difficult thing that the king requests, and *there is no other who can tell it to the king except the gods, whose dwelling is not with flesh.'*" Verses 10, 11.

After the wise men had thus confessed their inability to do what the king required, who offered to interpret the dream?

"So *Daniel* went in and asked the king to give him time, that he might tell the king the interpretation." Verse 16.

After Daniel and his fellows had sought God earnestly, how were the dream and its interpretation revealed to Daniel?

"Then the secret was revealed to Daniel *in a night vision.* So Daniel blessed the God of heaven." Verse 19.

When he was brought before the king, what did Daniel say?

"Daniel answered in the presence of the king, and said, 'The secret which the king has demanded, the wise men, the astrologers, the magicians, and the soothsayers cannot declare to the king. But *there is a God in heaven who reveals secrets,* and He has made known to King Nebuchadnezzar what will be in the latter days." Verses 27, 28.

The Great Image

What did Daniel say the king had seen in his dream?

"You, O king, were watching; and behold, *a great image!* This great image, whose splendor was excellent, stood before you; and its form was awesome." Verses 28-31.

Of what were the different parts of the image composed?

"This image's head was of fine *gold,* its chest and arms of *silver,* its belly and thighs of *bronze,* its legs of *iron,* its feet *partly of iron and partly of clay.*" Verses 32, 33.

By what means was the image broken to pieces?

"You watched while a *stone* was cut out without hands, which struck the image on its feet of iron and clay, and broke them in pieces." Verse 34.

What became of the various parts of the image?

"Then the iron, the clay, the bronze, the silver, and the gold were crushed together, and *became like chaff from the summer threshing floors; the wind carried them away* so that no trace of them was found. And the stone that struck the image became a great mountain and filled the whole earth." Verse 35.

Daniel and the Interpretation

With what words did Daniel begin the interpretation of the dream?

"You, O king, are a king of kings. For the God of heaven has given you a kingdom, power, strength, and glory; and wherever the children of men dwell, or the beasts of the field and the birds of the heaven, He has given them into your hand, and has made you ruler over them all—*you are this head of gold.*" Verses 37, 38.

NOTE—The character of the Neo-Babylonian Empire is fittingly indicated by the nature of the material composing that portion of the image by which it was symbolized—the head of gold. It was "the gold kingdom of a golden age." The metropolis, Babylon, as enlarged and beautified during the reign of Nebuchadnezzar, reached a height of unrivaled magnificence. The ancient writers, like Herodotus, are found by archaeologists to be generally accurate, except for a tendency to exaggerate as to size in their enthusiastic descriptions of the great city with its massive fortifications, its tower, and its "hanging gardens" rising terrace upon terrace, which came to be known among the Greeks as one of the Seven Wonders of the Ancient World.

Bible Answers

What was to be the nature of the next kingdom after Babylon?

"But after you shall arise another kingdom *inferior to yours.*" Verse 39.

Who was the last Babylonian king?

"That very night *Belshazzar,* king of the Chaldeans, was slain. And Darius the Mede received the kingdom, being about sixty-two years old." Daniel 5:30, 31. (See also verses 1, 2.)

To whom was Belshazzar's kingdom given?

"Your kingdom has been divided, and given to *the Medes and Persians.*" Verse 28.

By what is this kingdom of the Medes and Persians, generally known as the Persian Empire, represented in the great image?

The breast and arms of *silver.* (Daniel 2:32.)

By what is the Greek, or Macedonian, Empire, which succeeded the kingdom of the Medes and Persians, represented in the image?

"Its belly and thighs of *bronze.*" Verse 32. "But after you shall arise another kingdom inferior to yours; then another, a *third kingdom of bronze,* which shall rule over all the earth." Verse 39.

NOTE—That the empire that replaced the Persian was the Greek is clearly stated in Daniel 8:5-8, 20, 21.

What is said of the fourth kingdom?

"And the fourth kingdom *shall be as strong as iron,* inasmuch as iron breaks in pieces and shatters everything; and like iron that crushes, *that kingdom will break in pieces and crush all the others.*" Daniel 2:40.

What scripture shows that the Roman emperors ruled the world?

"And it came to pass in those days that *a decree went out from Caesar Augustus that all the world should be registered.*" Luke 2:1.

NOTE—Describing the Roman conquests, Edward Gibbon uses the very imagery employed in the vision of Daniel 2. He says: "The arms of the republic, sometimes vanquished in battle, always victorious in war, advanced with rapid steps to the Euphrates, the Danube, the Rhine, and the ocean; and the images of gold, or silver, or brass, that might serve to represent the nations and their kings, were successively broken by the iron monarchy of Rome" (*The History of the Decline and Fall of the Roman Empire,* "General Observations" [between chaps. 38 and 39], par. 1).

Humanity's Failure to Unite Nations

What was indicated by the mixture of clay and iron in the feet and toes of the image?

"Whereas you saw the feet and toes, partly of potter's clay and partly of iron, *the kingdom shall be divided;* yet the strength of the iron shall be in it, just as you saw the iron mixed with ceramic clay." Daniel 2:41.

NOTE—The barbarian tribes that overran the Roman Empire formed the kingdoms that developed into the nations of modern Europe.

Were any efforts to be made to reunite the divided empire of Rome?

"As you saw iron mixed with ceramic clay, *they will mingle with the seed of men;* but they will not adhere to one another, just as iron does not mix with clay." Verse 43.

NOTE—Charlemagne, Charles V, Louis XIV, Napoleon, Kaiser Wilhelm, and Hitler all tried to reunite the broken fragments of the Roman Empire and failed. *By marriage and intermarriage of royalty ties* have been formed with a view to strengthening and cementing together the shattered kingdom, but none have succeeded. The element of disunion remains. Many political revolutions and territorial changes have occurred in Europe since the end of the Western Roman Empire in A.D. 476; but its divided state still remains.

What is to take place in the days of these kingdoms?

"And in the days of these kings *the God of heaven will set up a kingdom which shall never be destroyed;* and the kingdom shall not be left to other people; it shall break in pieces and consume all these kingdoms, and it shall stand forever." Verse 44.

NOTE—This verse foretells the establishment of another universal kingdom, the kingdom of God. This kingdom is to overthrow and supplant all existing earthly kingdoms, and is to stand forever. The time for the setting up of this kingdom was to be "in the days of these kings." This cannot refer to the four preceding empires, or kingdoms, for they were not contemporaneous, but successive; neither can it refer to an establishment of the kingdom of Christ's first advent, for the 10 kingdoms that arose out of the ruins of the Roman Empire were not yet in existence. This final kingdom, then, is yet future.

In what announcement in the New Testament is the establishment of the kingdom of God made known?

"Then the seventh angel sounded: And there were loud voices in heaven, saying, '*The kingdoms of this world have become the kingdoms of our Lord and of His Christ,* and He shall reign forever and ever!'" Revelation 11:15.

Chapter 2

The Good News About The Bible

By what name are the sacred writings of the Bible commonly known?

"Jesus said to them, 'Have you never read in *the Scriptures:* "The stone which the builders rejected has become the chief cornerstone. This was the Lord's doing, and it is marvelous in our eyes"?'" Matthew 21:42.

What other title is given this revelation of God?

"But He answered and said to them, 'My mother and My brothers are these who hear *the word of God* and do it.'" Luke 8:21.

NOTE—It is interesting to note that the word "Bible" does not occur in the Bible itself. It is derived from the Latin *biblia,* which came from the Greek *biblos,* meaning "book." The Greek word *biblos* in turn is derived from *byblos,* meaning "papyrus," the name of the material upon which ancient books were written. The Greeks called this writing material *byblos* because they obtained it from the Phoenician port of Byblos.

The Bible has 66 books and was written by 35 or 40 authors over a period of some 1,500 years. The books are called the "Word of God," or the "Scriptures." *Scriptures* means "writings."

The Manner in Which the Scriptures Were Given

How were the Scriptures given?

"All Scripture is *given by inspiration of God.*" 2 Timothy 3:16.

By whom were those who thus spoke for God directed?

"For prophecy never came by the will of man, but holy men of God spoke as they were moved *by the Holy Spirit.*" 2 Peter 1:21.

What specific instance is mentioned by Peter?

"Men and brethren, this Scripture had to be fulfilled, *which the Holy Spirit spoke before by the mouth of David concerning Judas,* who became a guide to those who arrested Jesus." Acts 1:16.

Who, therefore, did the speaking through these individuals?

"*God,* who at various times and in various ways spoke in time past to the fathers by the prophets." Hebrews 1:1.

The Purpose of the Scriptures

For what purpose were the Scriptures written?

"For whatever things were written before were written *for our learning,* that we through the patience and comfort of the Scriptures might have hope." Romans 15:4.

For what is all Scripture profitable?

"All Scripture is given by inspiration of God, and is profitable *for doctrine, for reproof, for correction, for instruction in righteousness.*" 2 Timothy 3:16.

What was God's design in thus giving the Scriptures?

"That the man of God may be complete, *thoroughly equipped for every good work.*" Verse 17.

What does God design that His Word shall be to us in this world of darkness, sin, and death?

"Your word is a *lamp* to my feet and a *light* to my path." Psalm 119:105.

The Divisions of the Scriptures

What three general divisions did Jesus refer to in the writings of the Old Testament?

"Then He said to them, 'These are the words which I spoke to you while I was still with you, that all things must be fulfilled which were written in *the Law of Moses* and *the Prophets* and *the Psalms* concerning Me.'" Luke 24:44.

NOTE—"The law of Moses" was a common Jewish term for the first five books of the Old Testament. In "the prophets" were included Isaiah, Jeremiah, Ezekiel, and the 12 minor prophets; also Joshua, Judges, 1 and 2 Samuel, and 1 and 2 Kings. "The psalms" included all the remaining books.

Bible Answers

Upon what evidence did Jesus base His Messiahship?

"And beginning at *Moses* and all the *Prophets,* He expounded to them *in all the Scriptures* the things concerning Himself." Verse 27.

NOTE—Jesus referred particularly to the Old Testament prophecies as proof of His Messiahship. When Christ spoke of the Scriptures, He meant the Old Testament, for the New Testament had not yet been written.

The Character of God and His Word

What is God called in the Scriptures?

"He is the Rock, His work is perfect; for all His ways are justice, *a God of truth* and without injustice; righteous and upright is He." Deuteronomy 32:4.

What, therefore, must be the character of His Word?

"Sanctify them by Your truth. *Your word is truth.*" John 17:17.

To what extent has God magnified His Word?

"I will worship toward Your holy temple, and praise Your name for Your lovingkindness and Your truth; for You have magnified Your word *above all Your name.*" Psalm 138:2.

NOTE—A person's name stands for their character. It is the same with God. When God places His Word above His name, His character becomes the foundation of His Word and the pledge that His Word will be fulfilled. (Hebrews 6:13, 14.)

The Testimony of Job and Isaiah

What estimate did Job place upon the words of God?

"I have not departed from the commandment of His lips; *I have treasured the words of His mouth more than my necessary food.*" Job 23:12.

How firm was the faith of the great Isaiah in the Word of God?

"The grass withers, the flower fades, but *the word of our God stands forever.*" Isaiah 40:8.

The Power of God's Word in Nature

Through what agency did God create the heavens?

"*By the word of the Lord* the heavens were made, and all the host of them *by the breath of His mouth.* . . . For He

spoke, and it was done; *He commanded,* and it stood fast." Psalm 33:6-9.

By what does Christ uphold all things?

"Who being the brightness of His glory and the express image of His person, and upholding all things *by the word of His power.*" Hebrews 1:3.

Of what are some willingly ignorant?

"For this they willfully forget: that *by the word of God the heavens were of old,* and the earth standing out of water and in the water, *by which the world that then existed perished, being flooded with water.*" 2 Peter 3:5, 6.

By what are the present heavens and earth reserved for a similar fate?

"But the heavens and the earth which are now preserved *by the same word,* are reserved for fire until the day of judgment and perdition of ungodly men." Verse 7.

In what other scripture is it shown that creative power is exercised through the Word of God?

"Let them praise the name of the Lord, *for He commanded and they were created.*" Psalm 148:5.

Power of God's Word in Redemption

What change is wrought in one who is in Christ?

"Therefore, if anyone is in Christ, *he is a new creation;* old things have passed away; behold, *all things have become new.*" 2 Corinthians 5:17.

In what other words is this experience described by Jesus?

"Jesus answered and said to him, 'Most assuredly, I say to you, unless one is *born again,* he cannot see the kingdom of God.'" John 3:3.

Through what agency is this new creation, or new birth, accomplished?

"Having been born again, not of corruptible seed but incorruptible, *through the word of God* which lives *and abides forever.*" 1 Peter 1:23.

Natural and Spiritual Light Compared

What is the first creative commandment recorded in the Bible? And what was the result of it?

"Then God said, *'Let there be light';* and *there was light.*" Genesis 1:3.

What connection is there between the creation of light in the beginning, and the light of the gospel?

"For it is the God who commanded light to shine out of darkness, who has shone in our hearts to give *the light of the knowledge of the glory of God in the face of Jesus Christ.*" 2 Corinthians 4:6.

Amazing Power of the Word Spoken

Why were the people astonished at Christ's teaching?

"And they were astonished at His teaching, *for His word was with authority.*" Luke 4:32.

What testified to the power of the Word of Christ?

"Then they were all amazed and spoke among themselves, saying, 'What a word this is! For *with authority and power He commands the unclean spirits, and they come out.*'" Verse 36.

How did God heal His people anciently?

"*He sent His word and healed them,* and delivered them from their destructions." Psalm 107:20.

How did the centurion show his faith in Christ?

"The centurion answered and said, 'Lord, I am not worthy that You should come under my roof. But *only speak a word, and my servant will be healed.*'" Matthew 8:8.

The Seed of God's Word Working in Us

What did Christ say is the seed of the kingdom of God?

"The seed is *the word of God.*" Luke 8:11.

Where should the Word of Christ dwell?

"Let the word of Christ *dwell in you* richly in *all wisdom.*" Colossians 3:16.

What did Christ say of the unbelieving Jews respecting the Word of God?

"*But you do not have His word abiding in you,* because whom He sent, Him you do not believe." John 5:38.

How does the Word of God work in the believer?

"For this reason we also thank God without ceasing, because when you received the word of God which you heard from us, you welcomed it not as the word of men, but as it is in truth, the word of God, *which also effectively works in you who believe.*" 1 Thessalonians 2:13.

Heart Results of God's Word

What nature is imparted through the promises of God?

"By which have been given to us exceedingly great and precious promises, *that through these you may be partakers of the divine nature,* having escaped the corruption that is in the world through lust." 2 Peter 1:4.

By what are believers made clean?

"You are already clean *because of the word which I have spoken to you.*" John 15:3.

How does David say that a young man may cleanse his way?

"How can a young man cleanse his way? *By taking heed according to Your word.*" Psalm 119:9.

What power has the Word when hidden in the heart?

"Your word I have hidden in my heart, *that I might not sin against You.*" Psalm 119:11. (See also Psalm 17:4.)

General References to Christ

Of whom did Christ say the Scriptures testify?

"You search the Scriptures, for in them you think you have eternal life; and *these are they which testify of Me.*" John 5:39.

NOTE—"Search the Old Testament Scriptures: for they are they that testify of Christ. To find Him in them is the true and legitimate end of their study. To be able to interpret them as He interpreted them is the best result of all biblical learning."—Dean Alford.

Of whom did Moses and the prophets write?

"Philip found Nathanael and said to him, 'We have found Him of whom Moses in the law, and also the prophets, wrote—Jesus of Nazareth, son of Joseph.'" John 1:45.

NOTE—In her translation of the Old Testament Scriptures, Helen Spurrell expressed the following wish for all who should read her translation: "May very many exclaim, as the translator has often done when studying numerous passages in the original, *I have found the Messiah!*"

From whose words did Christ say the disciples ought to have learned of His death and resurrection?

"O foolish ones, and slow of heart to believe in all that *the prophets* have spoken! Ought not the Christ to have suffered these things and to enter into His glory?" Luke 24:25, 26.

How did Christ make it clear to them that the Scriptures testify of Him?

"And beginning at Moses and all the Prophets, *He expounded to them in all the Scriptures the things concerning Himself.*" Verse 27.

Christ the Seed

Where do we find the first promise of a Redeemer?

"So the Lord God said to the serpent: '. . . you shall eat dust all the days of your life. And I will put enmity between you and the woman, and between your seed and *her Seed; He shall bruise your head, and you shall bruise His heel.*'" Genesis 3:14, 15.

In what words was this promise renewed to Abraham?

"*In your seed* all the nations of the earth shall be blessed." Genesis 22:18. (See also Genesis 26:4; 28:14.)

To whom did this promised seed refer?

"Now to Abraham and his Seed were the promises made. He does not say, 'And to seeds,' as of many, but as of one, 'And to your Seed,' *who is Christ.*" Galatians 3:16.

The Angel and the Rock

Whom did God promise to send with Israel to guide them into the Promised Land?

"Behold, I send *an Angel* before you to keep you in the way and to bring you into the place which I have prepared." Exodus 23:20.

Who was the Rock that went with them?

"And all drank the same spiritual drink. For they drank of that spiritual Rock that followed them, and *that Rock was Christ.*" 1 Corinthians 10:4.

Birth, Life, Suffering, Death, Resurrection

Where was the Savior to be born?

"But you, *Bethlehem* Ephrathah, though you are little among the thousands of Judah, yet *out of you shall come forth* to Me the One to be Ruler in Israel, whose goings forth are from of old, from everlasting." Micah 5:2.

In what prophecy are Christ's life, suffering, and death touchingly foretold?

In the fifty-third chapter of Isaiah.

Where is the price of Christ's betrayal foretold?

"So they weighed out for my wages *thirty pieces of silver.*" Zechariah 11:12. (See Matthew 26:15.)

Where in the Psalms are Christ's dying words recorded?

"My God, My God, why have You forsaken Me?" Psalm 22:1. (See Matthew 27:46.) "Into Your hand I commit my spirit." Psalm 31:5. (See Luke 23:46.)

How is Christ's resurrection foretold in the Psalms?

"For *You will not leave my soul in Sheol,* nor will You allow Your Holy One to see corruption." Psalm 16:10. (See Acts 2:25-31.)

Christ's Second Coming and Kingdom

In what words does Daniel foretell Christ's receiving His kingdom?

"I was watching in the night visions, and behold, One like *the Son of Man,* coming with the clouds of heaven! He came to the Ancient of Days, and they brought Him near before Him. Then *to Him was given dominion and glory and a kingdom,* that all peoples, nations, and languages should serve Him. His dominion is an everlasting dominion, which shall not pass away, and His kingdom the one which shall not be destroyed." Daniel 7:13, 14. (See also Luke 1:32, 33; 19:11, 12; Revelation 11:15.)

How is Christ's second coming described in the Psalms?

"Let the rivers clap their hands; let the hills be joyful together before the Lord, *for He is coming to judge the earth. With righteousness He shall judge the world, and the peoples with equity.*" Psalm 98:8, 9. "*Our God shall come, and shall not keep silent; a fire shall devour before Him, and it shall be very tempestuous all around Him. He shall call to the heavens from above, and to the earth, that He may judge His people:* 'Gather My saints together to Me, those who have made a covenant with Me by sacrifice.'" Psalm 50:3-5.

Chapter 3

The Good News About
God

What two basic characteristics are part of God's nature?

"The Lord is *righteous* in all His ways, *gracious* in all His works." Psalm 145:17.

Does Christ possess these same attributes?

"By His knowledge *My righteous Servant* [Christ] shall justify many." Isaiah 53:11. "Nor will You allow *Your Holy One* to see corruption." Acts 2:27.

In what language is the justice of God described?

"He is the Rock, His work is perfect; for *all His ways are justice,* a God of truth and without injustice; *righteous and upright is He.*" Deuteronomy 32:4.

His Strength, Wisdom, and Faithfulness

What is said of the strength and wisdom of God?

"Behold, God is *mighty,* but despises no one; He is *mighty in strength of understanding.*" Job 36:5.

What treasures are hid in Christ?

"In whom are hidden all the treasures of *wisdom* and *knowledge.*" Colossians 2:3.

What is said of God's faithfulness in keeping His promises?

"Therefore know that the Lord your God, He is God, *the faithful God* who keeps covenant and mercy for a thousand generations." Deuteronomy 7:9.

The Love and Compassion of God

In what one word is the character of God expressed?

"He who does not love does not know God, for God is *love.*" 1 John 4:8.

What is said of the tender compassion of God?

"But You, O Lord, are a God *full of compassion,* and gracious, longsuffering and abundant in mercy and truth." Psalm 86:15.

His Gracious Impartiality

In what words is His impartiality proclaimed?

"For the Lord your God is God of gods and Lord of lords, the great God, mighty and awesome, *who shows no partiality* nor takes a bribe." Deuteronomy 10:17. "Then Peter opened his mouth and said: 'In truth I perceive that *God shows no partiality.* But in every nation whoever fears Him and works righteousness is accepted by Him.'" Acts 10:34, 35.

To how many is the Lord good?

"The Lord is *good to all,* and His tender mercies are over all His works." Psalm 145:9.

Why did Christ tell us to love our enemies?

"But I say to you, love your enemies, bless those who curse you, do good to those who hate you, and pray for those who spitefully use you and persecute you, *that you may be sons of your Father in heaven; for He makes His sun rise on the evil and on the good, and sends rain on the just and on the unjust.*" Matthew 5:44, 45.

Christ's Call to His People

How perfect does Christ tell His followers to be?

"Therefore you shall be perfect, *just as your Father in heaven is perfect.*" Verse 48.

What is God declared to be?

"God is *love.*" 1 John 4:16.

How great is God's love for the world?

"*For God so loved the world that He gave His only begotten Son,* that whoever believes in Him should not perish but have everlasting life." John 3:16.

In what act especially has God's love been manifested?

"In this the love of God was manifested toward us, that *God has sent His only begotten Son into the world, that we might live through Him.*" 1 John 4:9.

God's Delight

In what does God delight?

"Who is a God like You, pardoning iniquity and passing over the transgression of the remnant of His heritage? He does not retain His anger forever, because *He delights in mercy.*" Micah 7:18.

How are the mercies of Heaven continually manifested to us?

"Through the Lord's mercies we are not consumed, because His compassions fail not. *They are new every morning;* great is Your faithfulness." Lamentations 3:22, 23.

Upon how many does God bestow His blessings?

"He makes His sun rise on the evil and on the good, and sends rain on the just and on the unjust." Matthew 5:45.

In view of God's great love, what may we confidently expect?

"He who did not spare His own Son, but delivered Him up for us all, how shall He not with Him also freely *give us all things?*" Romans 8:32.

Fellowship and Trust

What did Jesus say of the one who loves Him?

"*He who loves Me will be loved by My Father,* and I will love him and manifest Myself to him." John 14:21.

Into what relationship to God does His love bring us?

"Behold what manner of love the Father has bestowed on us, that we should be called *children of God!*" 1 John 3:1.

As children of God, to what will we submit? How may we know that we are the children of God?

"For *as many as are led by the Spirit of God,* these are sons of God. . . . *The Spirit Himself bears witness with our spirit* that we are children of God." Romans 8:14-16.

How is the love of God supplied to the believer?

"Now hope does not disappoint, because the love of God has been poured out in our hearts *by the Holy Spirit* who was given to us." Romans 5:5.

Fellowship of Believers

In view of God's great love to us, what ought we to do?

"Beloved, if God so loved us, *we also ought to love one another.*" 1 John 4:11.

With what measure of love should we serve others?

"By this we know love, because He laid down His life for us. And *we also ought to lay down our lives for the brethren.*" 1 John 3:16.

What exhortation is based upon Christ's love for us?

"And *walk in love,* as Christ also has loved us and given Himself for us, an offering and a sacrifice to God for a sweet-smelling aroma." Ephesians 5:2.

Love's Wise Way

Upon what ground does God's work for sinners rest?

"But God, who is rich in mercy, because *of His great love with which He loved us,* even when we were dead in trespasses, made us alive together with Christ (by grace you have been saved), and raised *us up together, and made us sit together* in the heavenly places in Christ Jesus." Ephesians 2:4-6. (See Titus 3:5, 6.)

In what other way is God's love sometimes shown?

"For whom the Lord loves He *chastens,* and *scourges* every son whom He receives." Hebrews 12:6.

Love Everlasting

How enduring is God's love for us?

"The Lord has appeared of old to me, saying: 'Yes, *I have loved you with an everlasting love;* therefore with lovingkindness I have drawn you.'" Jeremiah. 31:3.

Can anything separate the true child of God from the love of God?

"For I am persuaded that neither death nor life, nor angels nor principalities nor powers, nor things present nor things to come, nor height nor depth, nor any other created thing, shall be able to separate us from the love of God which is in Christ Jesus our Lord." Romans 8:38, 39.

Chapter 4

The Good News About
The End of Sin and Suffering

The First Sinner

With whom did sin originate?

"He who sins is of the devil, *for the devil has sinned from the beginning.*" 1 John 3:8.

NOTE—Without the Bible, the question of the origin of evil would remain unexplained.

From what time has the devil been a murderer?

"You are of your father the devil, and the desires of your father you want to do. *He was a murderer from the beginning,* and does not stand in the truth, because there is no truth in him." John 8:44.

What is the devil's relationship to lying?

"When he speaks a lie, he speaks from his own resources, for *he is a liar and the father of it.*" Verse 44.

Was Satan created sinful?

"You were *perfect* in your ways from the day you were created, *till iniquity was found in you.*" Ezekiel 28:15.

NOTE—Ezekiel here refers to Satan under the figure "king of Tyre." (See verse 12.) This, and the statement in John 8:44, that he *"does* not stand in the truth," show that Satan was once *perfect,* and *in the truth.* Peter speaks of "the angels who *sinned*" (2 Peter 2:4), and Jude refers to "the angels who *did not keep their proper domain*" (Jude 6). These angels were once in a state of sinlessness.

What further statement of Christ seems to lay the responsibility for the origin of sin upon Satan and his angels?

"Then He will also say to those on the left hand, 'Depart from Me, you cursed, into the everlasting fire *prepared for the devil and his angels.*'" Matthew 25:41.

Satan and Christ Contrasted

What led to Satan's sin, rebellion, and downfall?

"*Your heart was lifted up because of your beauty;* you corrupted your wisdom for the sake of your *splendor.*" Ezekiel 28:17. "For you have said in your heart: '*I will ascend into heaven, I will exalt my throne above the stars of God; I will also sit on the mount of the congregation on the farthest sides of the north; . . . I will be like the Most High.*'" Isaiah 14:13, 14.

NOTE—In a word, pride and self-exaltation led to Satan's downfall, and for these there is no justification or adequate excuse. "Pride goes before destruction, and a haughty spirit before a fall." Proverbs 16:18. Hence, while we may know of the origin, cause, character, and results of evil, no good or sufficient reason or excuse can be given for it. To excuse it is to justify it; and the moment it is justified, it ceases to be sin. All sin is a manifestation of selfishness in some form, and its results are the opposite of those prompted by love. The experiment of sin will result finally in its utter abandonment and banishment forever, by all created intelligences, throughout the entire universe of God. Only those who foolishly and persistently cling to sin will be destroyed with it. The wicked will then be destroyed, root and branch (Malachi 4:1), and the righteous shall "shine like the brightness of the firmament," and "like the stars forever and ever." Daniel 12:3.

In contrast with the pride and self-exaltation exhibited by Satan, what spirit did Christ manifest?

"Who, being in the form of God, did not consider it robbery to be equal with God, *but made Himself of no reputation,* taking the form of a *bondservant,* and coming in the likeness of *men.* And being found in appearance as a man, *He humbled Himself* and became obedient to the point of *death,* even *the death of the cross.*" Philippians 2:6-8.

After we had sinned, how did God show His love and His willingness to forgive?

"For God so loved the world that He gave His only begotten Son, that whoever believes in Him should not perish but have everlasting life." John 3:16.

Definition and Nature of Sin

What is sin declared to be?

"Whoever commits sin also commits lawlessness, and *sin is lawlessness.*" 1 John 3:4.

What precedes the manifestation of sin?

"Then, when *desire* has conceived, it gives birth to sin." James 1:15.

The Results of Sin

What is the final result, or fruit, of sin?

"And sin, when it is full-grown, brings forth *death*." Verse 15. "The wages of sin is *death*." Romans 6:23.

Upon how many of the human race did death pass as the result of Adam's transgression?

"Therefore, just as through one man sin entered the world, and death through sin, and thus *death spread to all men*, because all sinned." Romans 5:12. "In Adam *all die*." 1 Corinthians 15:22.

How were the earth itself and its vegetation affected by Adam's sin?

"*Cursed is the ground* for your sake; in toil you shall eat of it all the days of your life. *Both thorns and thistles it shall bring forth for you*." Genesis 3:17, 18.

What additional curse came as the result of the first murder?

"And [the Lord] said [to Cain], '. . . So now you are cursed from the earth, which has opened its mouth to receive your brother's blood from your hand. When you till the ground, it shall no longer yield its strength to you.'" Genesis 4:10-12.

What terrible judgment came in consequence of continued sin and transgression against God?

"So the Lord said, 'I will destroy man whom I have created from the face of the earth, both man and beast, creeping thing and birds of the air, for I am sorry that I have made them.'" "And God said to Noah, 'The end of all flesh has come before Me, for the earth is filled with violence through them; and behold, I will destroy them with the earth.'" "Noah was six hundred years old when the *floodwaters* were on the earth." "On that day *all the fountains of the great deep were broken up, and the windows of heaven were opened*." Genesis 6:7, 13; 7:6, 11.

After the Flood, what came in consequence of further apostasy from God?

"But the Lord came down to see the city and the tower which the sons of men had built. And the Lord said, 'Indeed the people are one and they all have one language, and this is what they begin to do; now nothing that they propose to do will be withheld from them. Come, let Us go down and there *confuse their language, that they may not understand one another's speech*.' So the Lord scattered them abroad from there over the face of all the earth, and they ceased building the city." Genesis 11:5-8.

Into what condition has sin brought the entire creation?

"For we know that the whole creation *groans* and *labors with birth pangs together* until now." Romans 8:22.

God's Delay in Destroying Sin

What explains God's apparent delay in dealing with sin?

"The Lord is not slack concerning His promise, as some count slackness, but is *longsuffering toward us*, not willing that any should perish but that all should come to repentance." 2 Peter 3:9.

What is God's attitude toward the sinner?

"'For *I have no pleasure in the death of one who dies*,' says the Lord God. 'Therefore turn and live!'" Ezekiel 18:32.

Can sinners free themselves from the dominion of sin?

"Can the Ethiopian change his skin or the leopard its spots? *Then may you also do good who are accustomed to do evil*." Jeremiah 13:23.

What place has the will in determining whether humans shall have life?

"And the Spirit and the bride say, 'Come!' And let him who hears say, 'Come!' And let him who thirsts come. *Whoever desires, let him take the water of life freely*." Revelation 22:17.

Christ, the Sinner, and Satan

To what extent has Christ suffered for sinners?

"But He was *wounded* for our transgressions, He was *bruised* for our iniquities; the *chastisement* for our peace was upon Him, and by His *stripes* we are healed." Isaiah 53:5.

For what purpose was Christ manifested?

"And you know that *He was manifested to take away our sins*, and in Him there is no sin. . . . He who sins is of the devil, for the devil has sinned from the beginning. For this purpose the Son of God was manifested, *that He might destroy the works of the devil*." 1 John 3:5-8.

What was one direct purpose of the incarnation of Christ?

"Inasmuch then as the children have partaken of flesh and blood, He Himself likewise shared in the same, *that through death He might destroy him who had the power of death, that is, the devil.*" Hebrews 2:14.

The End of Sin and Sorrow

What triumphant chorus will mark the end of the reign of sin?

"And every creature which is in heaven and on the earth and under the earth and such as are in the sea, and all that are in them, I heard saying: *'Blessing and honor and glory and power be to Him who sits on the throne, and to the Lamb, forever and ever!'*" Revelation 5:13.

When and by what means will the effects of sin be removed?

"But the day of the Lord will come as a thief in the night, in which the heavens will pass away with a great noise, and *the elements will melt with fervent heat; both the earth and the works that are in it will be burned up.*" 2 Peter 3:10.

How thoroughly will the effects of sin be removed?

"And God will *wipe away every tear* from their eyes; there shall be *no more death, nor sorrow, nor crying. There shall be no more pain, for the former things have passed away.*" Revelation 21:4. "*And there shall be no more curse,* but the throne of God and of the Lamb shall be in it [the Holy City], and His servants shall serve Him." Revelation 22:3.

Will sin and its evil results ever appear again?

"There shall be *no more death.*" "And there shall be *no more curse.*" Revelation 21:4; 22:3.

God moves in a mysterious way
    His wonders to perform;
He plants His footsteps in the sea,
    And rides upon the storm.

Deep in unfathomable mines
    Of never-failing skill,
He treasures up His bright designs,
    And works His sovereign will.

Ye fearful saints fresh courage take;
    The clouds ye so much dread
Are big with mercy, and shall break
    In blessings on your head.

Judge not the Lord by feeble sense,
    But trust Him for His grace;
Behind a frowning providence
    He hides a smiling face.

His purpose will ripen fast,
    Unfolding every hour;
The bud may have a bitter taste,
    But sweet will be the flower.

Blind unbelief is sure to err,
    And scan His work in vain:
God is His own interpreter,
    And He will make it plain.
           —William Cowper

Chapter 5

The Good News About
The Man Who Was God

The Father's Testimony

How has the Father shown that His Son is one person of the Godhead?

"But *to the Son* He says: 'Your throne, *O God,* is forever and ever; a scepter of righteousness is the scepter of Your kingdom.'" Hebrews 1:8.

How was He recognized by the Father while on earth?

"And suddenly a voice came from heaven, saying, *'This is My beloved Son,* in whom I am well pleased.'" Matthew 3:17.

Christ's Testimony

In what way did Christ refer to the eternity of His being?

"And now, O Father, glorify Me together with Yourself, with the glory which I had with You *before the world was.*" John 17:5. "But you, Bethlehem Ephrathah, though you are little among the thousands of Judah, yet out of you shall come forth to Me the One to be Ruler in Israel, whose goings forth are from of old, *from everlasting.*" Micah 5:2. (See margin, and Matthew 2:6; John 8:58; Exodus 3:13, 14.)

What does Christ say is His relation to the Father?

"I and My Father are *one.*" John 10:30.

How did Christ assert an equal proprietorship with His Father in the kingdom?

"The Son of Man will send out His angels, and they will gather out of *His kingdom* all things that offend, and those who practice lawlessness." Matthew 13:41.

To whom do the elect equally belong?

"And shall God not avenge *His own elect* who cry out day and night to Him, though He bears long with them?" Luke 18:7. "And He [the Son of man] will send His angels with a great sound of a trumpet, and they will gather together *His elect* from the four winds, from one end of heaven to the other." Matthew 24:31.

Who are equally joined in bestowing the final rewards?

"But without faith it is impossible to please Him [God the Father], for he who comes to God must believe that He is, and that *He is a rewarder of those who diligently seek Him.*" Hebrews 11:6. "For the Son of Man will come in the glory of His Father with His angels, and *then He will reward each according to his works.*" Matthew 16:27.

NOTE—In the texts (Matthew 16:27; 13:41; 24:31) in which Christ refers to the angels as "His angels" and to the kingdom as "His kingdom" and to the elect as "His elect," He refers to Himself as "the Son of Man." It thus appears that while He was on earth as a man, He recognized His essential deity and His equality with His Father in heaven.

What does God declare Himself to be?

"Thus says the Lord, the King of Israel, and his Redeemer, the Lord of hosts: 'I am the *First* and I am the *Last;* besides Me there is no God.'" Isaiah 44:6.

In what scripture does Christ adopt the same expression?

"And behold, I am coming quickly, and My reward is with Me, to give to every one according to his work. I am the Alpha and the Omega, the Beginning and the End, the *First* and the *Last.*" Revelation 22:12, 13.

Apostles John and Paul Speak

What scripture states that the Son of God was God manifested in the flesh?

"In the beginning was the Word, and the Word was with God, and *the Word was God.*" "And *the Word became flesh* and dwelt among us, and we beheld His glory, the glory as of the only begotten of the Father, full of grace and truth." John 1:1, 14.

What fullness dwells in Christ?

"For in Him dwells *all the fullness of the Godhead bodily.*" Colossians 2:9.

Bible Answers

Christ the Savior

How was He manifested on earth as a Savior?

"For there is *born* to you this day in the city of David a Savior, who is Christ the Lord." Luke 2:11.

How was Christ begotten in the flesh?

"And the angel answered and said to her, '*The Holy Spirit* will come upon you, and *the power of the Highest* will overshadow you; therefore, also, that Holy One who is to be born will be called the Son of God.'" Luke 1:35.

Why was it necessary that He should be born thus, and partake of human nature?

"Therefore, in all things He had to be made like His brethren, *that He might be a merciful and faithful High Priest in things pertaining to God,* to make propitiation for the sins of the people." Hebrews 2:17.

Because we have such a wonderful Savior, what are we exhorted to do?

"Seeing then that we have a great High Priest who has passed through the heavens, Jesus the Son of God, *let us hold fast our confession.* For we do not have a High Priest who cannot sympathize with our weaknesses, but was in all points tempted as we are, yet without sin." Hebrews 4:14, 15.

Chapter 6

The Good News About
Our Future Home

Eternal Life and How to Obtain It

What precious promise has God made to His children?

"And this is the promise that He has promised us—*eternal life.*" 1 John 2:25.

How may we obtain eternal life?

"For God so loved the world that He gave His only begotten Son, *that whoever believes in Him should not perish but have everlasting life.*" John 3:16.

Who has everlasting life?

"*He who believes in the Son has everlasting life.*" Verse 36.

Where is this everlasting or eternal life?

"And this is the testimony: that God has given us eternal life, and *this life is in His Son.*" 1 John 5:11.

What therefore follows?

"*He who has the Son has life;* he who does not have the Son of God does not have life." Verse 12.

What does Christ give His followers?

"And I give them *eternal life,* and they shall never perish." John 10:28.

The Tree of Life, Past and Future

Why, after the Fall, were human beings shut away from the tree of life?

"*Lest [they] . . . take also of the tree of life, and eat, and live forever.*" Genesis 3:22.

What has Christ promised overcomers?

"To [them] who [overcomes] I will give *to eat from the tree of life,* which is in the midst of the Paradise of God." Revelation 2:7.

When Saints Become Immortal

When will immortality be conferred upon the saints?

"We shall not all sleep, but we shall all be changed—in a moment, in the twinkling of an eye, at the last trumpet. For the trumpet will sound, and the dead will be raised incorruptible, and we shall be changed. For this corruptible must put on incorruption, and this mortal must put on immortality." 1 Corinthians 15:51-53.

NOTE—In accepting Christ, believers receive "that eternal life, which was with the Father," and this eternal life they retain as long as Christ dwells in their hearts by faith. This wondrous gift may be lost by failure to maintain the faith that holds Christ fast. At the resurrection, immorality is conferred upon those who have fallen asleep in Christ, and thus the possession of eternal life becomes a permanent experience.

God's Purpose in Creation

For what purpose was the earth created?

"For thus says the Lord, who created the heavens, who is God, who formed the earth and made it, who has established it, who did not create it in vain, *who formed it to be inhabited:* 'I am the Lord, and there is no other.'" Isaiah 45:18.

To whom has God given the earth?

"The heaven, even the heavens, are the Lord's; but *the earth He has given to the children of men.*" Psalm 115:16.

For what purpose were human beings made?

"You have made [them] *to have dominion over the works of Your hands;* You have put all things under [their] feet." Psalm 8:6. (See Genesis 1:26; Hebrews 2:8.)

Satan and Humanity's Lost Dominion

How did human beings lose their dominion?

Through sin. (Romans 5:12; 6:23.)

When humans lost their dominion, to whom did they yield it?

"For by whom a person is overcome, by him also he is brought into bondage." 2 Peter 2:19.

NOTE—Humans were overcome by Satan in the Garden of Eden, and there yielded themselves and their possessions into the hands of their captor.

What ownership did Satan, in tempting Christ, claim?

"Then the devil, taking Him up on a high mountain, showed Him all the kingdoms of the world in a moment of time. And the devil said to Him, 'All this authority I will give You, and their glory; *for this has been delivered to me, and I give it to whomever I wish.*'" Luke 4:5, 6.

The Restored Dominion

What promise of restoration did the Lord make through Micah?

"And you, *O tower of the flock,* the stronghold of the daughter of Zion, *to you shall it come, even the former dominion* shall come, the kingdom of the daughter of Jerusalem." Micah 4:8.

Why did Christ say the meek are blessed?

"Blessed are the meek, *for they shall inherit the earth.*" Matthew 5:5.

NOTE—This inheritance cannot be realized in this life, for here the truly meek generally have little of earth's good things.

Who does the psalmist say have most now?

"For I was envious of the *boastful,* when I saw the prosperity of *the wicked. . . . Their eyes bulge with abundance; they have more than heart could wish.*" Psalm 73:3-7.

What promise was made to Abraham concerning the land?

"And the Lord said to Abram, after Lot had separated from him: 'Lift your eyes now and look from the place where you are—northward, southward, eastward, and westward; for *all the land which you see I give to you and your descendants forever.*'" Genesis 13:14, 15.

How much did this promise comprehend?

"*For the promise that he would be the heir of the world* was not to Abraham or to his seed through the law, but through the righteousness of faith." Romans 4:13.

How much of the land of Canaan did Abraham own in his lifetime?

"*And God gave him no inheritance in it, not even enough to set his foot on.* But even when Abraham had no child, He promised to give it to him for a possession, and to his descendants after him." Acts 7:5. (See Hebrews 11:13.)

How much of the promised possession did Abraham expect during his lifetime?

"By faith Abraham obeyed when he was called to go out to the place which he would receive as an inheritance. And he went out, not knowing where he was going. By faith *he dwelt in the land of promise as in a foreign country,* dwelling in tents with Isaac and Jacob, the heirs with him of the same promise; *for he waited for the city which has foundations, whose builder and maker is God.*" Hebrews 11:8-10.

Who is the seed to whom this promise was made?

"Now to Abraham and his Seed were the promises made. He does not say, 'And to seeds,' as of many, but as of one, '*And to your Seed,*' who is Christ." Galatians 3:16.

Who are heirs of the promise?

"And *if you are Christ's, then you are Abraham's seed, and heirs according to the promise.*" Verse 29.

Why did not these ancient worthies receive the promise?

"And all these, having obtained a good testimony through faith, did not receive the promise, God having provided something better for us, *that they should not be made perfect apart from us.*" Hebrews 11:39, 40.

When This Earth Is Made New

What is to become of our earth in the day of the Lord?

"But the day of the Lord will come as a thief in the night, in which the heavens will pass away with a great noise, and *the elements will melt with fervent heat; both the earth and the works that are in it will be burned up.*" 2 Peter 3:10.

What will follow this great conflagration?

"Nevertheless we, according to His promise, *look for new heavens and a new earth* in which righteousness dwells." Verse 13.

NOTE—As shown in the reading on the millennium, at the coming of Christ the living wicked will die, and the saints will be taken to heaven to dwell with Christ a thousand years, or until the wicked of all ages are judged and the time comes for the destruction and the purification of the earth by the fires of the last day. Following this, the earth will be formed anew, and humans, redeemed from sin, will be restored to their original dominion.

Bible Answers

To what Old Testament promise did Peter evidently refer?

"For behold, I create new heavens and a new earth; and the former shall not be remembered or come to mind." Isaiah 65:17.

What was shown the apostle John in vision?

"Now I saw *a new heaven and a new earth,* for the first heaven and the first earth had passed away. Also there was no more sea." Revelation 21:1.

How did Isaiah describe conditions on the "new earth"?

"They shall build houses and inhabit them; they shall plant vineyards and eat their fruit. They shall not build and another inhabit; they shall not plant and another eat; for as the days of a tree, so shall be the days of My people, and My elect shall long enjoy the work of their hands. They shall not labor in vain, nor bring forth children for trouble; for they shall be the descendants of the blessed of the Lord, and their offspring with them." Isaiah 65:21-23.

How readily will their wants be supplied?

"It shall come to pass that before they call, I will answer; and while they are still speaking, I will hear." Verse 24.

What peaceful condition will reign throughout the earth then?

"'The wolf and the lamb shall feed together, the lion shall eat straw like the ox, and dust shall be the serpent's food. They shall not hurt nor destroy in all My holy mountain,' says the Lord." Verse 25.

What seasons of worship will be observed in the new earth?

"'For as the new heavens and the new earth which I will make shall remain before Me,' says the Lord, 'so shall your descendants and your name remain. And it shall come to pass that *from one New Moon to another, and from one Sabbath to another,* all flesh shall come to worship before Me,' says the Lord." Isaiah 66:22, 23.

What will the ransomed of the Lord then do?

"*And the ransomed of the Lord shall return, and come to Zion with singing, with everlasting joy on their heads.* They shall obtain joy and gladness, and sorrow and sighing shall flee away." Isaiah 35:10.

A Real City

What was one of Christ's parting promises to His disciples?

"In My Father's house are many mansions; if it were not so, I would have told you. *I go to prepare a place for you.*" John 14:2.

What does Paul say God has prepared for His people?

"But now they desire a better, that is, a heavenly country. Therefore God is not ashamed to be called their God, for *He has prepared a city for them.*" Hebrews 11:16.

Where is this city, and what is it called?

"But the *Jerusalem above* is free, which is the mother of us all." Galatians 4:26.

For what did Abraham look?

"For *he waited for the city* which has foundations, whose builder and maker is God." Hebrews 11:10.

What assurance has God given to believers?

"Therefore God is not ashamed to be called their God, for He has prepared a city for them." Hebrews 11:16.

John Describes the City

What did John see concerning this city?

"Then *I, John, saw the holy city, New Jerusalem, coming down out of heaven from God,* prepared as a bride adorned for her husband." Revelation 21:2.

How many foundations has this city?

"Now the wall of the city had *twelve foundations,* and on them were the names of the twelve apostles of the Lamb." Verse 14.

What is the measurement of the city?

"The city is laid out as a square; its length is as great as its breadth. And *he measured the city with the reed: twelve thousand furlongs.*" Verse 16.

What is the height of the wall?

"Then he measured its wall: *one hundred and forty-four cubits.*" Verse 17.

NOTE—One hundred forty-four cubits are estimated at 216 feet in our measure.

Of what material is the wall constructed?

"The construction *of its wall was of jasper;* and the city was pure gold, like clear glass." Verse 18.

With what are the 12 foundations adorned?

"The foundations of the wall of the city were adorned with all kinds of precious stones: the first foundation was *jasper,* the second *sapphire,* the third *chalcedony,* the fourth *emerald,* the fifth *sardonyx,* the sixth *sardius,* the seventh chrysolite, the eighth *beryl,* the ninth *topaz,* the tenth *chrysoprase,* the eleventh *jacinth,* and the twelfth *amethyst."* Verses 19, 20. (See Exodus 28:15-21; Isaiah 54:11, 12.)

Of what are the 12 gates composed?

"The twelve gates were *twelve pearls:* each individual gate was of one pearl." Revelation 21:21.

What is written on these gates?

"The names of the twelve tribes of the children of Israel." Verse 12.

Of what does John say the streets of the city are composed?

"And the street of the city was *pure gold,* like transparent glass." Verse 21.

Why will this city have no need of the sun or moon?

"The city had no need of the sun or of the moon to shine in it, *for the glory of God illuminated it. The Lamb is its light.* And the nations of those who are saved shall walk in its light, and the kings of the earth bring their glory and honor into it." Verses 23, 24. (See Revelation 22:5; Isaiah 60:19, 20.)

Why are its gates not to be closed?

"Its gates shall not be shut at all by day *(there shall be no night there)."* Revelation 21:25.

Who May, and Who May Not, Enter

What will be excluded from this city?

"But there shall by no means enter it *anything that defiles, or causes an abomination or a lie."* Verse 27.

Who will be permitted to enter it?

"Blessed are those who do His commandments, that they may have the right to the tree of life, and may enter through the gates into the city." Revelation 22:14.

NOTE—The late English and American revisions render this, "Blessed are they that wash their robes," etc. The result is the same, for those who wash their robes cease to sin, and hence do God's commandments.

When this city becomes the metropolis of the new earth, what will be the condition of God's people?

"And God will wipe away every tear from their eyes; there shall be no more death, nor sorrow, nor crying. There shall be no more pain, for the former things have passed away." Revelation 21:4.

Everlasting Life and Glorious Privilege

What will flow through the city?

"And he showed me a *pure river of water of life,* clear as crystal, proceeding from the throne of God and of the Lamb." Revelation 22:1.

What stands on either side of the river?

"In the middle of its street, and on either side of the river, was *the tree of life,* which bore twelve fruits, each tree yielding its fruit every month. The leaves of the tree were for the healing of the nations." Verse 2.

NOTE—The tree of life, which Adam lost through transgression, is to be restored by Christ. Access to this is one of the promises to the overcomer. (Revelation 2:7.) Its bearing 12 kinds of fruit, a new kind each month, suggests a reason that in the new earth "from one *New Moon* to another," as well as "from one Sabbath to another," all flesh is to come before God to worship, as stated in Isaiah 66:22, 23.

Christ the Way of Life

What does Jesus declare Himself to be?

"Jesus said to him, *'I am the way, the truth, and the life.* No one comes to the Father except through Me.'" John 14:6.

Humanity's Situation

In what condition are all humans?

"But the Scripture has confined all *under sin,* that the promise by faith in Jesus Christ might be given to those who believe." Galatians 3:22. "For *all have sinned* and fall short of the glory of God." Romans 3:23.

What are the wages of sin?

"For the wages of sin is *death,* but the gift of God is eternal life in Christ Jesus our Lord." Romans 6:23.

How many are affected by Adam's transgression?

"Therefore, just as through one man sin entered the world, and death through sin, and thus *death spread to all men,* because all sinned." Romans 5:12.

When human beings first transgressed, what was done to prevent them from living forever in sin?

"Then the Lord God said, 'Behold, the man has become like one of Us, to know good and evil. And now, lest he put out his hand and take also of the tree of life, and eat, and live forever'—therefore *the Lord God sent him out* of the garden of Eden to till the ground from which he was taken. So He drove out the man; and He placed cherubim at the east of the garden of Eden, and a flaming sword which turned every way, to guard the way to the tree of life." Genesis 3:22-24.

God's Gift and Remedy

What is the gift of God?

"The gift of God is *eternal life* in Christ Jesus our Lord." Romans 6:23.

How many may receive this gift?

"And the Spirit and the bride say, 'Come!' And let him who hears say, 'Come!' And let him who thirsts come. *Whoever desires,* let him take the water of life freely." Revelation 22:17.

In whom is the gift?

"And this is the testimony: that God has given us eternal life, and *this life is in His Son.*" 1 John 5:11.

In receiving the Son, what do we have in Him?

"He who has the Son has *life.*" Verse 12.

What loss do those sustain who do not accept Him?

"He who does not have the Son of God *does not have life.*" Verse 12.

In what other way is this same truth stated?

"He who believes in the Son has everlasting life; and he who does not believe the Son shall not see life, but the wrath of God abides on him." John 3:36.

After one truly receives Christ, whose life will be manifested in that person?

"I have been crucified with Christ; it is no longer I who live, but *Christ lives in me;* and the life which I now live in the flesh I live by faith in the Son of God, who loved me and gave Himself for me." Galatians 2:20.

Spiritual Death and Rebirth

In what condition are all before they are quickened with Christ?

"But God, who is rich in mercy, because of His great love with which He loved us, even when we were *dead in trespasses,* made us alive together with Christ." Ephesians 2:4, 5.

What is this change from death to life called?

"Having been *born again,* not of corruptible seed but incorruptible, through the word of God which lives and abides forever." 1 Peter 1:23.

Salvation Through Faith

What is declared to be one purpose of Christ's death?

"Inasmuch then as the children have partaken of flesh and blood, He Himself likewise shared in the same, *that through death He might destroy him who had the power of death, that is, the devil.*" Hebrews 2:14.

Why have all been reckoned under sin?

"But the Scripture has confined all under sin, *that the promise by faith in Jesus Christ might be given to those who believe.*" Galatians 3:22.

How then do all become children of God?

"For you are all sons of God *through faith in Christ Jesus.*" Verse 26.

With whom are the children of God joint heirs?

"And if children, then heirs—heirs of God and *joint heirs with Christ.*" Romans 8:17.

Chapter 7

The Good News About
Salvation

Sin and Repentance

Who are called to repentance?

"I have not come to call the righteous, but *sinners,* to repentance." Luke 5:32.

What accompanies repentance?

"And that repentance and *remission of sins* should be preached in His name to all nations." Luke 24:47.

By what means is it made known?

"*By the law* is the knowledge of sin." Romans 3:20.

How many are sinners?

"For we have previously charged *both Jews and Greeks* that *they are all under sin.*" Verse 9.

What do transgressors bring upon themselves?

"Let no one deceive you with empty words, for because of these things *the wrath of God* comes upon the sons of disobedience." Ephesians 5:6.

Experiencing Salvation

Who awakens the soul to a sense of its sinful condition?

"And when He [*the Comforter*] *has come, He will convict* [literally, *"convince"*] *the world of sin.*" John 16:8.

What are fitting inquiries for those convicted?

"Men and brethren, *what shall we do?*" "Sirs, *what must I do to be saved?*" Acts 2:37; 16:30.

What replies does Inspiration return to these inquiries?

"*Repent, and let every one of you* be baptized in the name of Jesus Christ for the remission of sins." "*Believe on the Lord Jesus Christ,* and you will be saved." Acts 2:38; 16:31.

Fruits of True Repentance

What will the truly repentant sinner be constrained to do?

"I will *declare my iniquity;* I will be in *anguish* over my sin." Psalm 38:18.

What is the result of godly sorrow?

"For godly sorrow *produces repentance leading to salvation.*" 2 Corinthians 7:10.

What does the sorrow of the world do?

"The sorrow of the world *produces death.*" Verse 10.

How does godly sorrow for sin manifest itself?

"For observe this very thing, that you sorrowed in a godly manner: What *diligence* it produced in you, what *clearing of yourselves,* what indignation, what fear, what vehement desire, what zeal, what vindication! In all things you proved yourselves to be clear in this matter." Verse 11.

What did John the Baptist say to the Pharisees and Sadducees when he saw them come to his baptism?

"Brood of vipers! Who warned you to flee from the wrath to come?" Matthew 3:7.

What did he tell them to do?

"Therefore bear fruits worthy of repentance." Verse 8.

NOTE—There can be no true repentance without reformation. Repentance is a change of mind; reformation is a corresponding change of life.

When God sent the Ninevites a warning message, how did they show their repentance, and what was the result?

"Then God saw their works, that *they turned from their evil way; and God relented from the disaster that He had said He would bring upon them, and He did not do it.*" Jonah 3:10.

What leads sinners to repentance?

"Or do you despise the riches of His goodness, forbearance, and longsuffering, not knowing that *the goodness of God leads you to repentance?*" Romans 2:4.

Bible Answers

Confession and Forgiveness

What instruction is given concerning confession of sin?

"Speak to the children of Israel: 'When a man or woman commits any sin that men commit in unfaithfulness against the Lord, and that person is guilty, *then he shall confess the sin which he has committed.*'" Numbers 5:6, 7.

How futile is it to attempt to hide sin from God?

"But if you do not do so, then take note, you have sinned against the Lord; and *be sure your sin will find you out.*" Numbers 32:23. "You have set our iniquities before You, our secret sins in the light of Your countenance." Psalm 90:8. "And there is no creature hidden from His sight, but all things are naked and open to the eyes of Him to whom we must give account." Hebrews 4:13.

What promise is made to those who confess their sins?

"If we confess our sins, *He is faithful and just to forgive us our sins* and to cleanse us from all unrighteousness." 1 John 1:9.

What different results attend the covering and the confessing of sins?

"He who covers his sins *will not prosper,* but whoever confesses and forsakes them *will have mercy.*" Proverbs 28:13.

Being Definite in Confession

How definite should we be in confessing our sins?

"And it shall be, when he is guilty in any of these matters, that he shall confess that he has sinned *in that thing.*" Leviticus 5:5.

NOTE—"True confession is always of a specific character, and acknowledges particular sins. They may be of such a nature as to be brought before God only; they may be wrongs that should be confessed to individuals who have suffered injury through them; or they may be of a public character, and should then be as publicly confessed. But all confession should be definite and to the point, acknowledging the very sins of which you are guilty."—*Steps to Christ,* p. 38.

How fully did Israel once acknowledge their wrongdoing?

"And all the people said to Samuel, 'Pray for your servants to the Lord your God, that we may not die; for *we have added to all our sins the evil of asking a king for ourselves.*'" 1 Samuel 12:19.

When David confessed his sin, what did he say God did?

"I acknowledged my sin to You, and my iniquity I have not hidden. I said, 'I will confess my transgressions to the Lord,' and *You forgave the iniquity of my sin.*" Psalm 32:5.

God's Delight in Forgiving

What is God ready to do for all who seek for forgiveness?

"For You, Lord, are good, and *ready to forgive,* and abundant in mercy to all those who call upon You." Psalm 86:5.

Upon what did David rest his hope of forgiveness?

"Have mercy upon me, O God, *according to Your lovingkindness; according to the multitude of Your tender mercies,* blot out my transgressions." Psalm 51:1.

What is the measure of the greatness of God's mercy?

"For *as the heavens are high above the earth,* so great is His mercy toward those who fear Him." Psalm 103:11.

How fully does the Lord pardon when one repents?

"Let the wicked forsake his way, and the unrighteous man his thoughts; let him return to the Lord, and He will have mercy on him; and to our God, for *He will abundantly pardon.*" Isaiah 55:7.

What reason is given for God's readiness to forgive sin?

"Who is a God like You, pardoning iniquity and passing over *the transgression of the remnant of His heritage? He does not retain His anger forever, because He delights in mercy.*" Micah 7:18. (See Psalm 78:38.)

Why does God manifest such mercy and longsuffering toward those who seem to be holding on to sin?

"The Lord is not slack concerning His promise, as some count slackness, but is longsuffering toward us, *not willing that any should perish* but that all should come to repentance." 2 Peter 3:9.

Specific Examples

When the prodigal son, in the parable, repented and turned toward home, what did the father do?

"And he arose and came to his father. But when he was still a great way off, his father saw him and *had compassion,* and ran and fell on his neck and kissed him." Luke 15:20.

How did the father show his joy at his son's return?

"But the father said to his servants, *'Bring out the best robe*

and put it on him, and put a ring on his hand and sandals on his feet. And *bring the fatted calf here and kill it,* and let us eat and be merry; for this my son was dead and is alive again; he was lost and is found.'" Verses 22-24.

What is felt in heaven when a sinner repents?

"Likewise, I say to you, *there is joy in the presence of the angels of God* over one sinner who repents." Verse 10.

What did Hezekiah say God had done with his sins?

"Indeed it was for my own peace that I had great bitterness; but You have lovingly delivered my soul from the pit of corruption, for *You have cast all my sins behind Your back.*" Isaiah 38:17.

How completely does God wish to separate sin from us?

"You will cast all our sins into the depths of the sea." Micah 7:19. "As far as the east is from the west, so far has He removed our transgressions from us." Psalm 103:12.

How did the people respond to the preaching of John?

"Then Jerusalem, all Judea, and all the region around the Jordan went out to him and were baptized by him in the Jordan, *confessing their sins.*" Matthew 3:5, 6.

How did some of the believers at Ephesus testify to the sincerity of the confession of their sins?

"And many who had believed came *confessing and telling their deeds.* Also, many of those who had practiced magic *brought their books together and burned them in the sight of all.* And they counted up the value of them, and it totaled fifty thousand pieces of silver." Acts 19:18, 19.

Conditions of Forgiveness

Upon what basis has Christ taught us to ask forgiveness?

"And forgive us our debts, *as we forgive our debtors.*" Matthew 6:12.

What spirit must those cherish whom God forgives?

"For *if you forgive men their trespasses,* your heavenly Father will also forgive you. But if you do not forgive men their trespasses, neither will your Father forgive your trespasses." Verses 14, 15.

What exhortation is based on the fact that God has forgiven us?

"And be kind to one another, tenderhearted, *forgiving one another,* even as God in Christ forgave you." Ephesians 4:32.

The Blessed Giver and Receiver

Through whom are repentance and forgiveness granted?

"The God of our fathers raised up Jesus whom you murdered by hanging on a tree. Him God has exalted to His right hand to be Prince and Savior, *to give repentance* to Israel and *forgiveness of sins.*" Acts 5:30, 31.

In what condition is one whose sins are forgiven?

"*Blessed* is he whose transgression is forgiven, whose sin is covered. Blessed is the man to whom the Lord does not impute iniquity, and in whose spirit there is no deceit." Psalm 32:1, 2.

The Good News About
Living for Christ

Necessity of Conversion

How did Jesus emphasize the necessity of conversion?

"And said, 'Assuredly, I say to you, *unless you are converted* and become as little children, *you will by no means enter the kingdom of heaven.'*" Matthew 18:3.

In what other statement did He teach the same truth?

"Jesus answered and said to him, 'Most assuredly, I say to you, *unless one is born again,* he cannot see the kingdom of God.'" John 3:3.

How did He further explain the new birth?

"Jesus answered, 'Most assuredly, I say to you, *unless one is born of water and the Spirit,* he cannot enter the kingdom of God.'" Verse 5.

With what comparison did He illustrate the subject?

"*The wind* blows where it wishes, and you hear the sound of it, but cannot tell where it comes from and where it goes. *So is everyone who is born of the Spirit.*" Verse 8.

Agency of the New Creation

What takes place when one is converted to Christ?

"Therefore, if anyone is in Christ, *he is a new creation;* old things have passed away; behold, all things have become new." 2 Corinthians 5:17. (See Acts 9:1-22; 22:1-21; 26:1-23.)

What is the value of merely outward forms?

"For in Christ Jesus *neither circumcision nor uncircumcision avails anything,* but a new creation." Galatians 6:15.

Through what was the original creation wrought?

"*By the word of the Lord* the heavens were made, and all the host of them by the breath of His mouth." Psalm 33:6.

Through what instrumentality is conversion wrought?

"Having been born again, not of corruptible seed but incorruptible, *through the word of God* which lives and abides forever." 1 Peter 1:23.

Results of True Conversion

What change is wrought in conversion, or the new birth?

"Even when we were dead in trespasses, *made us alive* together with Christ (by grace you have been saved)." Ephesians 2:5.

What is one evidence of this change from death to life?

"We know that we have passed from death to life, *because we love the brethren.* He who does not love his brother abides in death." 1 John 3:14.

From what is a converted sinner saved?

"Let him know that he who turns a sinner from the error of his way will save a soul from *death* and cover a multitude of sins." James 5:20. (See Acts 26:14-18.)

To whom are sinners brought by conversion?

"Create in me a clean heart, O God, and renew a steadfast spirit within me. . . . Then I will teach transgressors Your ways, and sinners shall be *converted to You.*" Psalm 51:10-13.

In what words to Peter did Jesus indicate the kind of service a converted person should render to others?

"And the Lord said, 'Simon, Simon! Indeed, Satan has asked for you, that he may sift you as wheat. But I have prayed for you, that your faith should not fail; and *when you have returned to Me, strengthen your brethren.*'" Luke 22:31, 32.

What other experience is associated with conversion?

"For the hearts of this people have grown dull. Their ears are hard of hearing, and their eyes they have closed, lest they should see with their eyes and hear with their ears, lest they should understand with their hearts and *turn,* so that I should *heal them.*" Matthew 13:15.

What gracious promise does God make to His people?

"*I will heal their backsliding,* I will love them freely, for My anger has turned away from him." Hosea 14:4.

By what means is this healing accomplished?

"But He [Christ] was wounded for our transgressions,

Bible Answers

He was bruised for our iniquities; the chastisement for our peace was upon Him, and *by His stripes we are healed.*" Isaiah 53:5.

What are the evidences that one has been born of God?

"If you know that He is righteous, you know that everyone *who practices righteousness is born of Him.*" "Beloved, let us love one another, for love is of God; and *everyone who loves is born of God* and knows God." 1 John 2:29; 4:7.

What indwelling power keeps such from sinning?

"Whoever has been born of God does not sin, for *His* [God's] *seed remains in him;* and he cannot sin, because he has been born of God." 1 John 3:9. (See 1 John 5:4; Genesis 39:9.)

What will be the experience of those born of the Spirit?

"There is therefore now *no condemnation* to those who are in Christ Jesus, who do not walk according to the flesh, but according to the Spirit." Romans 8:1.

Believing and Beholding Jesus

What is true of everyone who believes in Jesus?

"Whoever believes that Jesus is the Christ is *born of God.*" 1 John 5:1.

What change is wrought by beholding Jesus?

"But we all, with unveiled face, beholding as in a mirror the glory of the Lord, are being *transformed into the same image* from glory to glory, just as by the Spirit of the Lord." 2 Corinthians 3:18.

NOTE—We were slaves to sin. Jesus came down and suffered with us and for us, and delivered us. As we behold Him in His Word and in prayer and meditation, and serve Him in the person of others, we may be changed more and more into the glory of His likeness; then, if faithful, we shall someday see Him "face to face."

The Good News About
The End of the World

Jerusalem's Destruction and Its Meaning

How did Christ feel concerning Jerusalem?

"Now as He drew near, He saw the city and *wept over it,* saying, 'If you had known, even you, especially in this your day, the things that make for your peace! But now they are hidden from your eyes.'" Luke 19:41, 42.

In what words did He foretell its destruction?

"For days will come upon you when your enemies will build an embankment around you, surround you and close you in on every side, and level you, and your children within you, to the ground; and they will not leave in you one stone upon another, because you did not know the time of your visitation." Verses 43, 44.

What appeal did He make to the impenitent city?

"O Jerusalem, Jerusalem, the one who kills the prophets and stones those who are sent to her! How often I wanted to gather your children together, as a hen gathers her chicks under her wings, but you were not willing!" Matthew 23:37.

As He was about to leave the Temple, what did He say?

"See! Your house is left to you *desolate.*" Verse 38.

NOTE—The Jews filled up their cup of iniquity by their final rejection and crucifixion of Christ, and their persecution of His followers after His resurrection. (See Matthew 23:29-35; John 19:15; Acts 4-8.)

What question did the disciples, upon hearing these words, ask?

"Tell us, when will these things be? And what will be the sign of Your coming, and of the end of the age?" Matthew 24:3.

NOTE—The overthrow of Jerusalem and of the Jewish nation is a type of the final destruction of all the cities of the world, and of all nations. The descriptions of the two events seem to be blended. Christ's prophetic words reached beyond Jerusalem's destruction to the final conflagration; they were spoken not for the early disciples only, but for those who were to live during the closing scenes of the world's history. Christ gave definite signs, both of the destruction of Jerusalem and of His second coming.

Did Christ indicate that either event was imminent?

"And Jesus answered and said to them: *'Take heed that no one deceives you.* For many will come in My name, saying, "I am the Christ," and will deceive many. And you will hear of wars and rumors of wars. See that you are not troubled; *for all these things must come to pass, but the end is not yet.'*" Verses 4-6.

What did He say of the wars, famines, pestilences, and earthquakes that were to precede these events?

"All these are *the beginning of sorrows.*" Verse 8.

NOTE—These were to precede and culminate in the overthrow, first, of Jerusalem, and finally of the whole world; for, as already noted, the prophecy has a double application, first, to Jerusalem and the Jewish nation, and second, to the whole world; the destruction of Jerusalem for its rejection of Christ at His first coming being a type of the destruction of the world at the end for its rejection of Christ in refusing to heed the closing warning message sent by God to prepare the world for Christ's second advent.

What would be the experiences of His people?

"Then they will deliver you up to tribulation and kill you, and you will be hated by all nations for My name's sake. And then many will be offended, will betray one another, and will hate one another. Then many false prophets will rise up and deceive many. And because lawlessness will abound, the love of many will grow cold." Verses 9-12.

Who did He say would be saved?

"But *he who endures to the end* shall be saved." Verse 13.

When did Christ say the end would come?

"And *this gospel of the kingdom will be preached in all the world as a witness to all the nations, and then the end will come.*" Verse 14.

NOTE—Before the fall of Jerusalem, Paul carried the gospel to Rome—then the capital of the world, he wrote of the

saints of "Caesar's household" (Philippians 4:22), and further said that the gospel had been "preached to every creature under heaven." Colossians 1:23.

Thus it was respecting the end of the Jewish nation; and thus it will be in the end of the world as a whole. When the gospel, or good news, of Christ's coming kingdom has been preached in all the world for a witness unto all nations, then the end will come. As the end of the Jewish nation came with overwhelming destruction, so will come the end of the world.

What would be a sign of the fall of Jerusalem?

"But *when you see Jerusalem surrounded by armies,* then know that its desolation is near." Luke 21:20.

At this time what were the disciples to do?

"Therefore when you see the 'abomination of desolation,' spoken of by Daniel the prophet, standing in the holy place (whoever reads, let him understand), then let those who are in Judea *flee to the mountains.*" Matthew 24:15, 16.

NOTE—In A.D. 66, when Cestius came against the city, but unaccountably withdrew, the Christians discerned in this the sign foretold by Christ, and fled (Eusebius, *Church History,* book 3, chap. 5), while 1.1 million Jews are said to have been killed in the terrible siege in A.D. 70. Here is a striking lesson on the importance of studying the prophecies and heeding the signs of the times. Those who believed Christ and watched for the signs that He had foretold were saved, while the unbelieving perished. So in the end of the world the watchful and believing will be delivered, while the careless and unbelieving will be snared and taken. (See Matthew 24:36-44; Luke 21:34-36; 1 Thessalonians 5:1-6.)

When the sign appeared, how suddenly were they to flee?

"Let him who is on the housetop not go down to take anything out of his house. And let him who is in the field not go back to get his clothes." Matthew 24:17, 18.

How did Christ further show His care for His disciples?

"And pray that your flight may not be in winter or on *the Sabbath.*" Verse 20.

NOTE—Flight in winter would entail discomfort and hardship; an attempt to flee on the Sabbath would doubtless meet with difficulty. The prayers of Christ's followers were heard. Events were so overruled that neither Jews nor Romans hindered their flight. When Cestius retreated, the Jews pursued his army, and the Christians thus had an opportunity to leave the city. The country was cleared of enemies, for at the

time of this siege, the Jews had assembled at Jerusalem for the Feast of Tabernacles. Thus the Christians of Judea were able to escape unmolested, and in the autumn, a most favorable time for flight.

What trying experience did Christ then foretell?

"For then *there will be great tribulation,* such as has not been since the beginning of the world until this time, no, nor ever shall be." Verse 21.

NOTE—In the siege of Jerusalem a prophecy of Moses (Deuteronomy 28:53) was literally fulfilled: "You shall eat the fruit of your own body, the flesh of your sons and your daughters . . . , in the siege and desperate straits in which your enemy shall distress you." For the fulfillment, see Josephus, *Wars of the Jews,* book 6, chap. 3, par. 4.

Following the destruction of Jerusalem came the persecution of the Christians under pagan emperors during the first three centuries of the Christian Era. Later came the greater and more terrible persecution during the long centuries of papal supremacy, foretold in Daniel 7:25 and Revelation 12:6. All these tribulations occurred under either pagan or papal Rome.

For whose sake would the period be shortened?

"And unless those days were shortened, no flesh would be saved; but *for the elect's sake those days will be shortened.*" Matthew 24:22.

NOTE—Through the influence of the Reformation of the sixteenth century, and the movements which grew out of it, the power of the Papacy to enforce its decrees against those it pronounced heretics was gradually lessened, until persecution ceased almost wholly by the middle of the eighteenth century, before the 1260 years ended.

Against what deceptions did Christ then warn us?

"Then if anyone says to you, 'Look, here is the Christ!' or 'There!' do not believe it. For false christs and false prophets will rise and show great signs and wonders to deceive, if possible, even the elect." Verses 23, 24.

Signs in Sun, Moon, and Stars

What signs of the end would be seen in the heavens?

"And *there will be signs in the sun, in the moon,* and *in the stars.*" Luke 21:25.

When were the first of these signs to appear?

"*Immediately after the tribulation of those days the sun will be darkened, and the moon will not give its light; the stars will fall from heaven, and the powers of the heavens will be shaken.*" Matthew 24:29. "But *in those days, after that tribulation,* the sun will be darkened, and the moon will not give its light; the stars of heaven will fall, and the powers in the heavens will be shaken." Mark 13:24, 25. Compare Joel 2:30, 31; 3:15; Isaiah 13:10; Amos 8:9.

NOTE—Within the 1260 years, but after the persecution (about the middle of the eighteenth century), the signs of His coming began to appear.

1. A *wonderful darkening of the sun and moon.* The remarkable Dark Day of May 19, 1780, is described by Samuel Williams of Harvard. The professor relates that the obscuration approached with the clouds from the southwest "between the hours of ten and eleven A.M., and continued until the middle of the next night," varying in degree and duration in different localities. In some places "persons could not see to read common print in the open air, for several hours," although "this was not generally the case." "Candles were lighted up in the houses;—the birds having sung their evening songs, disappeared, and became silent;—the fowls retired to roost;—the cocks were crowing all around, as at break of day;—objects could not be distinguished but at a very little distance; and everything bore the appearance and gloom of night." (See *Memoirs of the American Academy of Arts and Sciences* [through 1783], vol. 1, pp. 234, 235.)

Since the moon, full the night before, was on the opposite side of the earth, there was no eclipse of the sun—nor could an eclipse last so long. The causes assigned seem inadequate to account for the area covered.

"The darkness *of the following evening* was probably as gross as ever has been observed since the Almighty fiat gave birth to light. It wanted only palpability to render it as extraordinary, as that which overspread the land of Egypt in the days of Moses. . . . If every luminous body in the universe had been shrouded in impenetrable shades, or struck out of existence, the darkness could not have been more complete. A sheet of white paper held within a few inches of the eyes was equally invisible with the blackest velvet."—Samuel Tenney, Letter (1785), in *Collections of the Massachusetts Historical Society* (1792 ed.), part 1, vol. 1, pp. 97, 98. (Italics supplied.)

Timothy Dwight, president of Yale, remembered that "a very general opinion prevailed, that the day of judgment was at hand. The [Connecticut] House of Representatives, being unable to transact their business, adjourned," but the Council lighted candles, preferring, as a member said, to be found at work if the judgment were approaching. (See John W. Barber, *Connecticut Historical Collections* [2nd ed., 1836], p. 403.)

There was no agreement among the current writers as to the cause of this unparalleled darkness, but there was entire agreement as to the extraordinary character of it. Any suggestion of a natural cause or causes for the darkness can in no wise militate against the significance of the event. Sixteen and a half centuries before it occurred the Savior had definitely foretold this twofold sign, saying, "But in those days, after that tribulation, the sun will be darkened, and the moon will not give its light." Mark 13:24. These signs occurred exactly as predicted, and at the time indicated so long before their occurrence. It is this fact, and not the cause of the darkness, that is significant in this connection. When the Lord would open a path for His people through the sea, He did it by "a strong east wind." Exodus 14:21. Was it for this reason any less miraculous? When the bitter waters were made sweet (Exodus 15:23-25), was the divine interposition any less real because certain natural means were used, having apparently some part, under divine direction, in rendering the water fit for drinking? In like manner, even though it were possible for science to account for the remarkable darkness of May 19, 1780, instead of merely speculating concerning it, the event would not be discredited thereby as a merciful sign of the approaching end of probationary time.

2. *Remarkable display of falling stars.* "The morning of November 13th, 1833," says an eyewitness, a Yale astronomer, "was rendered memorable by an exhibition of the phenomenon called shooting stars, which was probably more extensive and magnificent than any similar one hitherto recorded. . . . Probably no celestial phenomenon has ever occurred in this country, since its first settlement, which was viewed with so much admiration and delight by one class of spectators, or with so much astonishment and fear by another class."—Denison Olmsted, in *The American Journal of Science and Arts* (1834), vol. 25, pp. 363, 364.

"From the Gulf of Mexico to Halifax, until daylight with some difficulty put an end to the display, the sky was scored in every direction with shining tracks and illuminated with majestic fireballs. At Boston, the frequency of meteors was estimated to be about half that of flakes of snow in an average snowstorm. . . . Traced backwards, their paths were invariably found to converge to a point in the constellation Leo."—Agnes M. Clerke, *A Popular History of Astronomy* (1885 ed.), pp. 369, 370.

Frederick Douglass, in reminiscing about his early days in slavery, says: "I witnessed this gorgeous spectacle, and was awe-struck. The air seemed filled with bright descending messengers from the sky. . . . I was not without the suggestion at the moment that it might be *the harbinger of the coming of the Son of Man;* and in my then state of mind I was prepared to hail Him as my friend and deliverer. I had read that 'the stars shall fall from heaven,' and they were now falling."—*Life and Times of Frederick Douglass* (1941 ed.), p. 117. (Italics supplied.)

World Conditions, Preparation

What were to be the signs on earth of Christ's coming?

"*Distress of nations,* with perplexity, *the sea and the waves roaring; men's hearts failing them from fear* and the expectation of those things which are coming on the earth." Luke 21:25, 26.

What was to be the next great event?

"Then they will see *the Son of Man coming in a cloud with power and great glory.*" Verse 27. (See Matthew 24:30.)

When these things begin to happen, what should we do?

"Now when these things begin to happen, *look up and lift up your heads,* because your redemption draws near." Luke 21:28.

When the trees put forth their leaves, what do we know?

"Now learn this parable from the fig tree: When its branch has already become tender and puts forth leaves, *you know that summer is near.*" Matthew 24:32.

What do we likewise know after these signs are seen?

"So you also, when you see all these things, *know that it is near—at the doors!*" Verse 33. "So you also, when you see these things happening, *know that the kingdom of God is near.*" Luke 21:31.

What did Christ say of the certainty of this prophecy?

"Assuredly, I say to you, this generation will by no means pass away till all these things take place. Heaven and earth will pass away, but My words will by no means pass away." Matthew 24: 34, 35.

NOTE—What Christ foretold of the destruction of Jerusalem came true to the very letter. Likewise may we be assured that what He has said about the end of the world will as certainly and as literally be fulfilled.

Who alone knows the exact day of Christ's coming?

"But of that day and hour *no one knows,* not even the angels of heaven, but *My Father only.*" Verse 36.

What moral conditions will precede Christ's second advent?

"But as the days of Noah were, so also will the coming of the Son of Man be. For as in the days before the flood, they were *eating* and *drinking, marrying* and *giving in marriage,* until the day that Noah entered the ark, and did not know until the flood came and took them all away, *so also will the coming of the Son of Man be.*" Verses 37-39.

What important admonition has Christ given us?

"Therefore you *also be ready,* for the Son of Man is coming at an hour you do not expect." Verse 44.

What will be the experience of those who say in their hearts that the Lord is not soon coming?

"But if that evil servant says in his heart, 'My master is delaying his coming,' and begins to beat his fellow servants, and to eat and drink with the drunkards, the master of that servant will come on a day when he is not looking for him and at an hour that he is not aware of, and will cut him in two and appoint him his portion with the hypocrites. There shall be weeping and gnashing of teeth." Verses 48-51.

Chapter 10

The Good News About
The Coming King

What promise did Christ make concerning His coming?

"Let not your heart be troubled; you believe in God, believe also in Me. In My Father's house are many mansions; if it were not so, I would have told you. I go to prepare a place for you. And if I go and prepare a place for you, *I will come again* and receive you to Myself; that where I am, there you may be also." John 14:1-3.

What follows the signs of Christ's coming?

"Then they will see *the Son of Man coming in a cloud with power and great glory.*" Luke 21:27.

Angels and Apostles Proclaim It

At His ascension, how was Christ's return promised?

"And while they looked steadfastly toward heaven as He went up, behold, two men stood by them in white apparel, who also said, 'Men of Galilee, why do you stand gazing up into heaven? *This same Jesus, who was taken up from you into heaven, will so come in like manner as you saw Him go into heaven.*'" Acts 1:10, 11.

How does Paul give expression to this hope?

"Looking for the blessed hope and glorious appearing of our great God and Savior Jesus Christ." Titus 2:13.

What is Peter's testimony regarding it?

"For we did not follow cunningly devised fables when we made known to you the power and coming of our Lord Jesus Christ, but were eyewitnesses of His majesty." 2 Peter 1:16.

The Unprepared

Will the inhabitants of the earth as a whole be prepared to meet Him?

"Then the sign of the Son of Man will appear in heaven, and *then all the tribes of the earth will mourn,* and they will see the Son of Man coming on the clouds of heaven with power and great glory." Matthew 24:30. "Behold, He is coming with clouds, and every eye will see Him, even they who pierced Him. And *all the tribes of the earth will mourn because of Him.*" Revelation 1:7.

Why will many not be prepared for this event?

"But if that evil servant says in his heart, *'My master is delaying his coming,'* and begins to beat his fellow servants, and to eat and drink with the drunkards, the master of that servant will come on a day when he is not looking for him and at an hour that he is not aware of, and will cut him in two and appoint him his portion with the hypocrites. There shall be weeping and gnashing of teeth." Matthew 24:48-51.

What will the world be doing when Christ comes?

"But as the days of Noah were, so also will the coming of the Son of Man be. 38 For as in the days before the flood, *they were eating and drinking, marrying and giving in marriage,* until the day that Noah entered the ark, and did not know until the flood came and took them all away, so also will the coming of the Son of Man be. Verses 37-39. "Likewise as it was also in the days of Lot: *They ate, they drank, they bought, they sold, they planted, they built;* but on the day that Lot went out of Sodom it rained fire and brimstone from heaven and destroyed them all. Even so will it be in the day when the Son of Man is revealed." Luke 17:28-30.

NOTE—These texts do not teach that it is wrong in itself to eat, drink, marry, buy, sell, plant, or build, but that people's minds will be so taken up with these things that they will give little to no thought to the future life, and make no plans or preparation to meet Jesus when He comes.

Who is it that blinds men to the gospel of Christ?

"Whose minds *the god of this age* [Satan] has blinded, who do not believe, lest the light of the gospel of the glory of Christ, who is the image of God, should shine on them." 2 Corinthians 4:4.

NOTE—"To my mind this precious doctrine—for such I must call it—of the return of the Lord to this earth is taught in the New Testament as clearly as any other doctrine in it; yet I was in the Church fifteen to sixteen years before I ever heard a sermon on it. There is hardly any church that doesn't make a great deal of baptism, but in all of Paul's epistles I believe baptism is only spoken of thirteen times, while it speaks about the return of our Lord fifty times; and yet the Church has had very little to say about it. Now, I can see a reason for this; the devil does not want us to see this truth, for nothing would wake up the Church so much. The moment a man takes hold of the truth that Jesus Christ is coming back again to receive his followers to himself, this world loses its hold upon him. Gas stocks and water stocks and stocks in banks and railroads are of very much less consequence to him then, his heart is free, and he looks for the blessed appearing of his Lord, who, at his coming, will take him into his blessed Kingdom."—D. L. Moody, *The Second Coming of Christ* (Revell), pp. 6, 7.

"'This same Jesus, which is taken up from you into heaven, *shall so come in like manner as ye have seen him go into heaven,*' is the parting promise of Jesus to his disciples, communicated through the two men in white apparel, as a cloud received him out of their sight. When after more than fifty years in glory he breaks the silence and speaks once more in the Revelation which he gave to his servant John, the post-ascension Gospel which he sends opens with, '*Behold, he cometh with clouds,*' and closes with '*Surely I come quickly.*' Considering the solemn emphasis thus laid upon this doctrine, and considering the great prominence given to it throughout the teaching of our Lord and of his apostles, how was it that for the first five years of my pastoral life it had absolutely no place in my preaching? Undoubtedly the reason lay in the lack of early instruction. Of all the sermons heard from childhood on, I do not remember listening to a single one upon the subject."—A. J. Gordon, *How Christ Came to Church,* pp. 44, 45. (Italics supplied.)

Prepared for His Coming

When are the saved to be like Jesus?

"Beloved, now we are children of God; and it has not yet been revealed what we shall be, but we know that *when He is revealed, we shall be like Him,* for we shall see Him as He is." 1 John 3:2.

Will Christ's coming be a time of reward?

"For the Son of Man will come in the glory of His Father with His angels, and *then He will reward each according to his works.*" Matthew 16:27. "And behold, I am coming quickly, *and My reward is with Me,* to give to every one according to his work." Revelation 22:12.

To whom is salvation promised at Christ's appearing?

"So Christ was offered once to bear the sins of many. *To those who eagerly wait for Him* He will appear a second time, apart from sin, for salvation.*" Hebrews 9:28.

What influence has this hope upon the life?

"Beloved, now we are children of God; and it has not yet been revealed what we shall be, but we know that when He is revealed, we shall be like Him, for we shall see Him as He is. And *everyone who has this hope in Him purifies himself, just as He is pure.*" 1 John 3:2, 3.

To whom is a crown of righteousness promised?

"For I am already being poured out as a drink offering, and the time of my departure is at hand. I have fought the good fight, I have finished the race, I have kept the faith. Finally, there is laid up for me the crown of righteousness, which the Lord, the righteous Judge, will give to me on that Day, and not to me only but also *to all who have loved His appearing.*" 2 Timothy 4:6-8.

What will the waiting ones say when Jesus comes?

"And it will be said in that day: 'Behold, this is our God; we have waited for Him, and He will save us. This is the Lord; we have waited for Him; we will be glad and rejoice in His salvation.'" Isaiah 25:9.

Has the exact time of Christ's coming been revealed?

"But of that day and hour *no one knows,* not even the angels of heaven, but My Father only." Matthew 24:36.

In view of this fact, what does Christ tell us to do?

"*Watch therefore,* for you do not know what hour your Lord is coming." Verse 42.

NOTE—"To the secure and careless he will come as a thief in the night: to his own, as their Lord."—Henry Alford, *The New Testament for English Readers,* vol. 1, part 1, p. 170. "The proper attitude of a Christian is to be always looking for his Lord's return."—D. L. Moody, *The Second Coming of Christ* (Revell), p. 9.

What warning has Christ given that we might not be taken by surprise by this great event?

"But take heed to yourselves, lest your hearts be weighed down with carousing, drunkenness, and cares of this life, and that Day come on you unexpectedly. For it will come as a snare on all those who dwell on the face of the whole earth. Watch therefore, and pray always that you may be counted worthy to escape all these things that will come to pass, and to stand before the Son of Man." Luke 21:34-36.

What Christian grace are we exhorted to exercise in our expectant longing for this event?

"Therefore be *patient,* brethren, until the coming of the Lord. See how the farmer waits for the precious fruit of the earth, waiting patiently for it until it receives the early and latter rain. You also be *patient*. Establish your hearts, for the coming of the Lord is at hand." James 5:7, 8.

What has been the general attitude of Christians toward the second coming of Christ?

The belief of the Christian church in the second coming of Christ appears in Christian literature from the origin of the so-called Apostles' Creed down through to very recent times.

NOTE—These creeds can be found in the classic work *The Creeds of Christendom* (Harper) by the great church historian Philip Schaff. From that work we quote but two examples:

"The Nicene Creed is the first which obtained universal authority. It rests on older forms used in different churches of the East, and has undergone again some changes. . . . The original Nicene Creed dates from the first ecumenical Council, which was held at Nicaea, A.D. 325."—Vol. 1, pp. 24, 25. The text from which we quote is the original text of A.D. 325:

"We believe in . . . one Lord Jesus Christ, . . . who . . . suffered, and the third day he rose again, ascended into heaven; from thence *He shall come* to judge the quick and the dead."—*Ibid.*, pp. 28, 29. (Italics supplied.)

The New Hampshire Baptist Confession (1833), which is "widely accepted by Baptists, especially in the Northern and Western States" (*ibid.*, vol. 3, p. 742), says:

"We believe that the end of the world is approaching; that *at the last day Christ will descend from Heaven, and raise the dead from the grave to final retribution;* that a solemn separation will then take place; that the wicked will be adjudged to endless punishment, and the righteous to endless joy; and that this judgment will fix forever the final state of men in heaven or hell, on principles of righteousness."—*Ibid.*, p. 748. (Italics supplied.)

Does Christ Come at Time of Death?

Did the early disciples think that death would be the second coming of Christ?

"Peter, seeing him [John], said to Jesus, 'But Lord, what about this man?' Jesus said to him, 'If I will that he remain *till I come,* what is that to you? You follow Me.' Then this saying went out among the brethren that this disciple *would not die.* Yet Jesus did not say to him that he would not die, but, 'If I will that he remain till I come, what is that to you?'" John 21:21-23.

NOTE—From this it is evident that the early disciples regarded death and the coming of Christ as two separate events. "'Therefore be ye also ready: for in such an hour as ye think

not the Son of man cometh.' Some people say that means death; but the Word of God does not say it means death. Death is our enemy, but our Lord hath the keys of Death; he has conquered death, hell and the grave. . . . Christ is the Prince of Life; there is no death where he is; death flees at his coming; dead bodies sprang to life when he touched them or spoke to them, his coming is not death; he is the resurrection and the life; when he sets up his kingdom there is to be no death, but life forevermore."—D. L. Moody, *The Second Coming of Christ* (Revell), pp. 10, 11.

Christ and Angels Testify

At Christ's ascension, how did the angels say He would come again?

"Now when He had spoken these things, while they watched, He was taken up, and *a cloud received Him out of their sight.* And while they looked steadfastly toward heaven as He went up, behold, two men stood by them in white apparel, who also said, 'Men of Galilee, why do you stand gazing up into heaven? This same Jesus, who was taken up from you into heaven, *will so come in like manner as you saw Him go into heaven.*'" Acts 1:9-11.

How did Christ Himself say He would come?

"For the Son of Man will come *in the glory of His Father with His angels.*" Matthew 16:27. "Then all the tribes of the earth will mourn, and they will see the Son of Man *coming on the clouds of heaven with power and great glory.*" Matthew 24:30.

Apostles John and Paul Speak

How many will see Him when He comes?

"Behold, He is coming with clouds, and *every eye will see Him,* even they who pierced Him." Revelation 1:7.

NOTE—Christ's second coming will be as real as was His first, and as visible as His ascension, and far more glorious. To spiritualize our Lord's return is to pervert the obvious meaning of His promise, "I will come again," and nullify the whole plan of redemption; for the reward of the faithful of all ages is to be given at this most glorious of all events.

What demonstration will accompany His coming?

"For the Lord Himself will descend from heaven with a shout, *with the voice of an archangel, and with the trumpet of God.* And the dead in Christ will rise first." 1 Thessalonians 4:16.

Jesus Warns of Deception

What warning has Christ given concerning false views?

"Then if anyone says to you, *'Look, here is the Christ!'* or *'There!' do not believe it.* For false christs and false prophets will rise and show great signs and wonders to deceive, if possible, even the elect. See, I have told you beforehand. Therefore if they say to you, 'Look, He is in the *desert!'* do not go out; or 'Look, He is in the inner rooms!' do not believe it." Matthew 24:23-26.

How visible is His coming to be?

"For as the lightning comes from the east and flashes to the west, so also will the coming of the Son of Man be." Verse 27.

Chapter 11

The Good News About
The Creator

How the Sabbath Was Made

When and by whom was the Sabbath made?

"Thus the heavens and the earth, and all the host of them, were finished. And *on the seventh day God ended His work* which He had done, *and He rested on the seventh day* from all His work which He had done." Genesis 2:1, 2.

What is the reason for keeping the Sabbath day holy?

"*For in six days the Lord made the heavens and the earth, the sea, and all that is in them, and rested the seventh day.* Therefore the Lord blessed the Sabbath day and hallowed it." Exodus 20:11.

NOTE—The Sabbath is the memorial of Creation, the sign of God's creative power. God designed that through keeping it human beings should forever remember Him as the true and living God, the Creator of all things.

On the perpetuity of the Sabbath command, Wesley declared, "'Six days shalt thou do all manner of work. But the seventh day is the Sabbath of the Lord thy God.' It is not thine, but God's day. He claims it for his own. He always did claim it for his own, even from the beginning of the world. 'In six days the Lord made heaven and earth, and rested the seventh day. Therefore the Lord blessed the Sabbath-day and hallowed it.' He *hallowed* it; that is, he made it holy; he reserved it for his own service. He appointed, that as long as the sun or the moon, the heavens and the earth, should endure, the children of men should spend this day in the worship of him who 'gave them life and breath and all things.'"—John Wesley, "A Word to a Sabbath-Breaker," in *Works* (1830 ed.), vol. 11, pp. 164-166. (Italics supplied.)

Did Christ have anything to do with Creation and the making of the Sabbath?

"All things were made *through Him,* and *without Him nothing was made that was made.*" John 1:3. (See also Ephesians 3:9; Colossians 1:16; Hebrews 1:2.)

NOTE—Christ was the active agent in creation. The Creator rested on the seventh day from the work of creation; therefore, Christ must have rested on the seventh day with the Father. Consequently, it is His rest day as well as the Father's.

After God rested on the seventh day, what did He do?

"Then God *blessed the seventh day and sanctified it,* because in it He rested from all His work which God had created and made." Genesis 2:3.

NOTE—By three distinct acts, then, was the Sabbath made: God *rested* on it; He *blessed* it; He *sanctified* it, *Sanctify* means "to make sacred or holy," "to consecrate," "to set apart as sacred."

Human Beings and the Sabbath

From whom did Christ say the Sabbath was made?

"And He said to them, '*The Sabbath was made for man, and not man for the Sabbath.*'" Mark 2:27.

NOTE—*Man* here means humanity. God instituted the Sabbath to be a source of benefit and blessing to the human family.

"Jesus says: 'The Sabbath was made for man;' and the necessary inference is that from the beginning man knew the primary uses of the day, and received the benefits which it was designed to impart. . . .

"Before the giving of the law from Sinai the obligation of the Sabbath was understood."—J. J. Taylor (Baptist), *The Sabbath Question* (Revell, 1914 ed.), pp. 20-24.

"I honestly believe that this commandment is just as binding today as it ever was. I have talked with men who have said that it has been abrogated, but they have never been able to point to any place in the Bible where God repealed it. When Christ was on earth, He did nothing to set it aside; He freed it from the traces under which the scribes and Pharisees had put it, and gave it its true place. 'The Sabbath was made for man, and not man for the Sabbath.' It is just as practicable and as necessary for men today as it ever was—in fact, more than ever, because we live in such an intense age.

"The sabbath was binding in Eden, and it has been in force ever since. This fourth commandment begins with the word 'remember,' showing that the sabbath already existed when God wrote this law on the tables of stone at Sinai. How can men claim that this one commandment has been done away with when they will admit that the other nine are still binding?"—D. L. Moody, *Weighed and Wanting* (1898 ed.), pp. 46, 47.

When did God bless and sanctify the seventh day?

"And on the seventh day God ended His work which He had done, and He rested on the seventh day from all His work which He had done. Then God blessed the seventh day and sanctified it, *because in it He rested from all His work* which God had created and made." Genesis 2:2, 3.

NOTE—"If we had no other passage than this of Genesis 2:3, there would be no difficulty in deducing from it a precept for the universal observance of a Sabbath, or seventh day, to be devoted to God as holy time, by all of that race for whom the earth and its nature were specially prepared. The first men must have known it. The words 'He hallowed it' can have no meaning otherwise. They would be a blank unless in reference to some who were required to keep it holy."—John Peter Lange, *A Commentary on the Holy Scriptures,* on Genesis 2:3, vol. 1, p. 197.

The Sabbath Test in Israel

What does the Sabbath commandment require?

"*Remember the Sabbath day, to keep it holy.* Six days you shall labor and do all your work, but the seventh day is the Sabbath of the Lord your God. *In it you shall do no work:* you, nor your son, nor your daughter, nor your male servant, nor your female servant, nor your cattle, nor your stranger who is within your gates." Exodus 20:8-10.

NOTE—Luther says, on Exodus 16:4, 22-30: "Hence you can see that the Sabbath was before the law of Moses came, and has existed from the beginning of the world. Especially have the devout who have preserved the true faith, met together and called upon God on this day."—Translated from *Auslegung des Alten Testaments* (Commentary on the Old Testament), in *Sämmtliche Schriften* (Collected Writings), edited by J. G. Walch, vol. 3, col. 950.

How did God prove Israel in the wilderness?

"*Behold, I will rain bread from heaven for you.* And the people shall go out and gather a certain quota every day, *that I may test them, whether they will walk in My law or not.*" Exodus 16:4.

On which day was a double portion of manna gathered?

"And so it was, *on the sixth day, that they gathered twice as much bread,* two omers for each one." Verse 22.

What did Moses say to the rulers?

"*This is what the Lord has said: 'Tomorrow is a Sabbath rest, a holy Sabbath to the Lord.'*" Verse 23.

NOTE—"2. The Sabbath is indispensable to man, being promotive of his highest good, physically, intellectually, socially, spiritually, and eternally. Hence its observance is connected with the best of promises, and its violation with the severest penalties. Ex. 23:12; 31:12-18; Neh. 13:15-22; Isa. 56:2-7; 58:13, 14; Jer. 17:21-27; Eze. 20:12, 13; 22:26-31. Its sanctity was very distinctly marked in the gathering of the manna. Ex. 16:22-30.

"3. The original law of the Sabbath was renewed and made a prominent part of the moral law, or ten commandments, given through Moses at Sinai. Ex. 20:8-11."—Amos Binney and Daniel Steele, *Binney's Theological Compend Improved* (1902 ed.), p. 170.

What did some of the people do on the seventh day?

"Now it happened that *some of the people went out on the seventh day to gather,* but they found none." Verse 27.

How did God reprove their disobedience?

"And the Lord said to Moses, *'How long do you refuse to keep My commandments and My laws?'*" Verse 28.

Why was twice as much manna given on the sixth day?

"See! *For the Lord has given you the Sabbath; therefore He gives you on the sixth day bread for two days.* Let every man remain in his place; let no man go out of his place on the seventh day." Verse 29.

How did the Lord test the people?

Over the keeping of the Sabbath.

NOTE—Thus we see that the Sabbath commandment was a part of God's law before this law was spoken from Sinai, for this incident occurred before Israel came to Sinai. Both the Sabbath and the law existed from Creation.

"As presented to us in the Scriptures the Sabbath was not the invention of any religious founder. It was not at first part of any system of religion, but an entirely independent institution. Very definitely it is presented in Genesis as the very first institution, inaugurated by the Creator himself. It was purely religious, wholly moral, wholly spiritual. It had no prescribed ceremonies, no sacramentarian significance. It required no priest, no liturgy. It was for man as God's creature, steward and friend."—W. O. Carver, *Sabbath Observance,* p. 41. Copyright 1940 by the Sunday School Board of the Southern Baptist Convention. Used by permission.

Bible Answers

God's Memorial

What is to endure throughout all generations?

"Your name, O Lord, endures forever, Your fame, O Lord, throughout all generations." Psalm 135:13. Memorial: "Anything . . . intended to preserve the memory of a person or event."—*Webster's Collegiate Dictionary* (5th ed., 1935), p. 624.

What illustration of a memorial is given in the Bible?

"So this day shall be to you a memorial; and you shall keep it as a feast to the Lord throughout your generations. You shall keep it as a feast by an everlasting ordinance." Exodus 12:14.

NOTE—This, the Passover, was a periodical memorial, to be observed on the fourteenth day of the first month of each year, the day on which the Israelites were delivered from Egyptian bondage, and its celebration was to be, with the seven days' feast of unleavened bread following and connected with it, in commemoration of that event. (See Exodus 13:3-9.)

God's Memorial of Creation

Did God design the Creation to be remembered?

"The works of the Lord are great, studied by all who have pleasure in them. His work is honorable and glorious, and His righteousness endures forever. He has made His wonderful works to be remembered." Psalm 111:2-4.

What has He commanded humanity to observe in memory of this great work?

"Remember the Sabbath day, to keep it holy. . . . For in six days the Lord made the heavens and the earth, the sea, and all that is in them, and rested the seventh day. Therefore the Lord blessed the Sabbath day and hallowed it." Exodus 20:8-11.

Of what was this memorial to be a sign?

"Hallow My Sabbaths, and they will be a sign between Me and you, that you may know that I am the Lord your God." Ezekiel 20:20.

How long was the Sabbath to a sign of the true God?

"It is a sign between Me and the children of Israel forever; for in six days the Lord made the heavens and the earth, and on the seventh day He rested and was refreshed." Exodus 31:17.

NOTE—It is manifest that if the object of the Sabbath was to remember God as the Creator, and if it had been faithfully kept from the first, there would not now be a heathen or an idolator on the face of the earth.

Bible Answers

What besides Creation were the Israelites to remember when they kept the Sabbath?

"And remember that you were a slave in the land of Egypt, and the Lord your God brought you out from there by a mighty hand and by an outstretched arm; therefore the Lord your God commanded you to keep the Sabbath day." Deuteronomy 5:15.

NOTE—There is a deep significance to this scripture. In Egypt, through oppression and idolatrous surroundings, the keeping of the Sabbath had become not only almost obsolete but well-nigh impossible. They were delivered from bondage in order that they might keep God's law (Psalm 105:43-45), and particularly the Sabbath, the great seal, sign, and memorial institution of the law. The recollection of their bondage and oppressed condition in Egypt was to be an additional incentive for keeping the Sabbath in the land of freedom. The Sabbath, therefore, besides being a memorial of Creation, was to be to them a memorial of their deliverance from bondage, and of the great power of God as manifested in this deliverance. And as Egypt stands as a symbol of the condition of everyone in the world under the slavery of sin, so the Sabbath is to be kept by every saved soul as a memorial of the deliverance from the slavery by the mighty power of God through Christ.

Of what else does God say He gave the Sabbath to His people to be a sign, or reminder?

"Moreover I also gave them My Sabbaths, to be a sign between them and Me, that they might know that I am the Lord who sanctifies them." Ezekiel 20:12.

NOTE—Sanctification is a work of redemption—of making holy sinful or unholy beings. Like the work of Creation itself, this requires power. (See Psalm 51:10; John 3:3, 6; Ephesians 2:10.) And as the Sabbath is the appropriate sign, or memorial, of the creative power of God wherever displayed, whether in Creation, deliverance from human bondage, or deliverance from the slavery of sin, it is to be kept as a sign of the work of sanctification. This will be one great reason for the saints keeping it throughout eternity. It will remind them not only of their own creation and the creation of the universe but also of their redemption.

Through whom do we have sanctification?

"But of Him you are in Christ Jesus, who became for us wisdom from God—and righteousness and sanctification and redemption." 1 Corinthians 1:30.

NOTE—Then, as the Sabbath is a sign, or memorial, of sanctification, and as Christ is the one through whom the work of sanctification is accomplished, the Sabbath is a sign, or memorial, of what Christ is to the believer. Through the Sabbath, therefore, God designed that the believer and Christ should be very closely linked together.

In heaven, how often will the redeemed congregate to worship the Lord?

"'For as the new heavens and the new earth which I will make shall remain before Me,' says the Lord, 'so shall your descendants and your name remain. And it shall come to pass that from one New Moon to another, and from one Sabbath to another, all flesh shall come to worship before Me,' says the Lord." Isaiah 66:22, 23.

NOTE—The Sabbath, which is the memorial of God's creative power, will never cease to exist. When this sinful state of things shall give way to the sinless new earth, the fact upon which the Sabbath institution is based will still remain; and those who shall be permitted to live in the new earth will still commemorate the creative power of God, while singing the song of Moses and the Lamb. (Revelation 15:3. See Revelation 22:1, 2.)

Maker and Keeper of the Sabbath

Of what did Christ say the Son of man is Lord?

"For the Son of Man is Lord even *of the Sabbath*." Matthew 12:8. (See also Mark 2:28.)

Who made the Sabbath?

"All things were made *through Him* [Christ, the Word]." John 1:3.

NOTE—Christ was the creative agent.

Did Christ, while on earth, keep the Sabbath?

"*As His custom was, He went into the synagogue on the Sabbath day, and stood up to read*." Luke 4:16.

Although Lord, Maker, and an observer of the Sabbath, how was Christ watched and spied upon on this day?

"So the scribes and Pharisees watched Him closely, *whether He would heal on the Sabbath*, that they might find an accusation against Him." Luke 6:7.

How did Christ meet their false ideas of Sabbathkeeping?

"Then Jesus said to them, '. . . *Is it lawful on the Sabbath to do good or to do evil, to save life or to destroy?*'" Verse 9.

How did they manifest their displeasure at His healing the

man with the withered hand on the Sabbath?

"But they were *filled with rage,* and *discussed with one another what they might do to Jesus.*" Verse 11. "Then the Pharisees went out and immediately *plotted* with the Herodians against Him, *how they might destroy Him.*" Mark 3:6.

NOTE—Although the miracle Christ performed had given evidence that He was from God, they were angry because He had shown *their views of Sabbathkeeping to be wrong.* Wounded pride, obstinacy, and malice, therefore, combined to fill them with *madness;* and they went out immediately and held counsel with the Herodians—their political enemies—for the purpose of accomplishing His death.

Because Jesus healed a man on the Sabbath day, and told him to take up his bed and walk, what did the Jews do?

"For this reason the Jews *persecuted* Jesus, and *sought to kill Him,* because He had done these things on the Sabbath." John 5:16.

NOTE—It is noteworthy that not the least of the malice that finally caused His crucifixion was engendered over this very question of Sabbath observance. Christ did not keep the Sabbath according to their ideas, and so they sought to kill Him. Many today cherish this same spirit. Because some do not agree with their idea of the Sabbath, or Sabbath observance, they seek to persecute and oppress them—seek laws, and alliances with political powers, to compel respect for their views.

How did Jesus answer them?

"But Jesus answered them, *'My Father has been working until now, and I have been working.'*" Verse 17.

NOTE—The ordinary operations of nature, as manifested in God's almighty, upholding, beneficent, and healing power, continue on the Sabbath. To cooperate with God and nature in the work of healing on the Sabbath cannot, therefore, be out of harmony with God's Sabbath law.

What effect did this answer have upon the Jews?

"Therefore the Jews *sought all the more to kill Him.*" Verse 18.

Because the disciples plucked a few heads of grain on the Sabbath day to satisfy hunger, what did the Pharisees say?

"And the Pharisees said to Him, *'Look, why do they do what is not lawful on the Sabbath?'*" Mark 2:24.

What was Christ's reply?

"But He said to them, 'Have you never read what David

did when he was in need and hungry, he and those with him: how he went into the house of God in the days of Abiathar the high priest, and ate the showbread, which is not lawful to eat except for the priests, and also gave some to those who were with him?' And He said to them, *'The Sabbath was made for man, and not man for the Sabbath.'*" Verses 25-27.

What was said of Christ's healing a woman one Sabbath?

"The ruler of the synagogue answered, . . . *'There are six days on which men ought to work; therefore come and be healed on them, and not on the Sabbath day.'*" Luke 13:14.

What was Christ's answer?

"The Lord then answered him and said, 'Hypocrite! Does not each one of you on the Sabbath loose his ox or donkey from the stall, and lead it away to water it? So ought not this woman, being a daughter of Abraham, whom Satan has bound—think of it—for eighteen years, be loosed from this bond on the Sabbath?'" Verses 15, 16.

What effect did Christ's answers have upon the people?

"And when He said these things, *all His adversaries were put to shame; and all the multitude rejoiced* for all the glorious things that were done by Him." Verse 17.

How did Christ justify acts of mercy on the Sabbath?

"What man is there among you who has one sheep, and if it falls into a pit on the Sabbath, will not lay hold of it and lift it out? Of how much more value then is a man than a sheep? Therefore it is lawful to do good on the Sabbath." Matthew 12:11, 12. (See also Luke 14:5, 6.)

NOTE—"Jesus observed the Sabbath Day of his own people. It was his custom to worship in the synagogues on the Sabbath Day. After he entered upon his own ministry, he and his followers continued to recognize and use the Sabbath Day, but according to his own individual and spiritual insight and interpretation. Even when Sabbath observance was made one of the chief grounds of bitter antagonism to him by the Pharisees he continued his recognition of the Sabbath and uttered no word that can properly be construed as lacking in deep reverence. Apparently, he expected that his followers would continue to hold and inculcate the spirit of the historic Sabbath."—W. O. Carver, *Sabbath Observance,* p. 25. Copyright 1940 by the Sunday School Board of the Southern Baptist Convention. Used by permission.

What dispute did Christ's miracles cause?

"Therefore some of the Pharisees said, *'This Man is not from God, because He does not keep the Sabbath.'* Others said, *'How can a man who is a sinner do such signs?'*" John 9:16.

Bible Answers

NOTE—By these miracles God was setting the seal of His approval to Christ's views and teachings respecting the Sabbath, and to His manner of observing it, and thus condemning the narrow and false views of the Pharisees. Hence the division.

Jesus Magnifies the Sabbath

According to Isaiah, what was Christ to do with the law?

"He will *exalt* the law and *make it honorable.*" Isaiah 42:21.

NOTE—In nothing, perhaps, was this more strikingly fulfilled than in the matter of Sabbath observance. By their numerous traditional regulations and senseless restrictions the Jews had made the Sabbath a burden, and anything but a delight. Christ removed all these, and by His life and teachings restored the Sabbath to its proper place as a day of worship, of contemplation of God, a day for doing acts of charity and mercy. Thus He magnified it and made it honorable. One of the most prominent features of Christ's ministry was this work of *Sabbath reform.* Christ did not *abolish* or *change* the Sabbath; but He did rescue it from the rubbish of tradition, false ideas, and superstitions by which it had been degraded. The Pharisees had placed the institution *above* humanity and *against* humanity. Christ reversed the order, and said, "The Sabbath was made *for man,* and not man *for the Sabbath.*" He showed that it was to minister to the happiness and well-being of both humans and other animals.

In view of the coming destruction and desolation of the city of Jerusalem, for what did Christ tell His disciples to pray?

"And pray that your flight may not be in winter *or on the Sabbath.*" Matthew 24:20.

NOTE—"Christ is here speaking of the flight of the apostles and other Christians out of Jerusalem and Judea, just before their final destruction, as is manifest by the whole context, and especially by the 16th verse: 'Then let them which be in Judea flee into the mountains.' But the final destruction of Jerusalem was after the dissolution of the Jewish constitution, and after the Christian dispensation was fully set up. Yet it is plainly implied in these words of the Lord, that even then Christians were bound to a strict observation of the Sabbath."—Jonathan Edwards, *Works* (reprint of Worcester ed., 1844-1848), vol. 4, pp. 621, 622.

"The Great Teacher never intimated that the Sabbath was a ceremonial ordinance to cease with the Mosaic ritual. . . . Instead of anticipating its extinction along with the ceremonial law, he speaks of its existence after the downfall of Jerusalem.

[See Matthew 24:20.]"—W. D. Killen (Irish Presbyterian), *The Ancient Church* (1883 ed.), p. 188.

Sabbath and the Cross

What day immediately precedes the first day of the week?

"Now after *the Sabbath,* as the first day of the week began to dawn, Mary Magdalene and the other Mary came to see the tomb." Matthew 28:1.

NOTE—According to the New Testament, therefore, the Sabbath had passed when the first day of the week began.

After the Crucifixion, what day was kept by the women who followed Jesus?

"Then they returned and prepared spices and fragrant oils. And they *rested on the Sabbath according to the commandment.*" Luke 23:56.

When is the Sabbath, "according to the commandment"?

"But *the seventh day is the Sabbath* of the Lord your God." Exodus 20:10.

Jesus and the Sabbath

What was Christ's custom respecting the Sabbath?

"So He came to Nazareth, where He had been brought up. And as His custom was, *He went into the synagogue on the Sabbath day,* and stood up to read." Luke 4:16.

In what instruction to His disciples did Christ recognize the existence of the Sabbath long after His ascension?

"And pray that your flight may not be in winter *or on the Sabbath.*" Matthew 24:20.

NOTE—The flight of the Christians took place late in October, A.D. 66, three and one-half years before the fall of Jerusalem. For Jesus' attitude toward the Sabbath, see the preceding reading.

Paul and the Sabbath

On what day did Paul and Barnabas preach at Antioch?

"They came to Antioch in Pisidia, and went into the synagogue on *the Sabbath day.*" Acts 13:14.

When did the Gentiles ask Paul to repeat his sermon?

"So when the Jews went out of the synagogue, the Gentiles

begged that these words might be preached to them *the next Sabbath.*" Verse 42.

On what day did Paul preach to the women at Philippi?

"And *on the Sabbath day* we went out of the city to the riverside, where prayer was customarily made; and we sat down and spoke to the women who met there." Acts 16:13.

On what day did Paul preach to the Jews at Thessalonica?

"Now when they had passed through Amphipolis and Apollonia, they came to Thessalonica, where there was a synagogue of the Jews. Then Paul, *as his custom was, went in to them, and for three Sabbaths reasoned with them from the Scriptures.*" Acts 17:1, 2.

NOTE—It was Paul's custom, as it was Christ's (Luke 4:16), to attend religious services on the Sabbath.

How did the apostle spend the working days of the week when at Corinth, and what did he do on the Sabbath?

"So, because he was of the same trade, he stayed with them and *worked;* for by occupation they were *tentmakers.*" Acts 18:3. (See Ezekiel 46:1.) "And *he reasoned in the synagogue every Sabbath,* and persuaded both Jews and Greeks." Acts 18:4.

NOTE—"And [Paul] continued there a year and six months, teaching the word of God among them." Verse 11. These texts do not definitely prove that the apostle held 78 Sabbath meetings in Corinth, but they show conclusively that it was his custom to observe that day by devoting it to religious purposes. The careful student will note that Paul's reasoning in the synagogue every Sabbath applies only to the comparatively brief time during which he was permitted the use of the synagogue. But the history of the apostle's work in the book of Acts fully warrants us in believing that wherever he was, Paul utilized to the full every opportunity to pursue his gospel work on the Sabbath. The same is true, not only of the apostles, but of most Christians during the first three centuries.

John and the Lord's Day

On what day was John in the Spirit?

"I was in the Spirit *on the Lord's Day.*" Revelation 1:10.

Who is Lord of the Sabbath?

"Therefore the Son of Man is also Lord of the Sabbath." Mark 2:28.

What, through Isaiah, does the Lord call the Sabbath?

"If you turn away your foot from the Sabbath, from doing your pleasure on *My holy day.*" Isaiah 58:13.

Why does the Lord call the Sabbath His day?

"For in six days the Lord made the heavens and the earth, the sea, and all that is in them, and *rested the seventh day.* Therefore the Lord blessed *the Sabbath day and hallowed it.*" Exodus 20:11.

Through whom did God create the world?

"God . . . has in these last days spoken to us *by His Son,* . . . through *whom also He made the worlds.*" Hebrews 1:1, 2.

NOTE—The Bible recognizes but one weekly Sabbath—the day upon which God rested in the beginning; which was made known to Israel at Sinai (Nehemiah 9:13, 14); was observed by Christ and His apostles; and is to be kept by the redeemed in the new earth (Isaiah 66:22, 23).

The terms *Sabbath, Sabbaths,* and *Sabbath days* occur 60 times in the New Testament, and in every case but one refer to the seventh day. In Colossians 2:16, 17, reference is made to the annual Sabbaths connected with the three annual feasts observed by Israel before the first coming of Christ.

"The sacred name of the seventh day is Sabbath. This fact is too clear to require argument. The truth is stated in concise terms: 'The seventh day is the Sabbath of the Lord thy God.' This utterance is repeated in Exodus 16:26; 23:12; 31:15; 35:2; Leviticus 23:3; and Deuteronomy 5:14. On this point the plain teaching of the word has been admitted in all ages. Except to certain special Sabbaths appointed in Levitical law, and these invariably governed by the month rather than the week, the Bible in all its utterances never, no, not once, applies the name Sabbath to any other day."—J. J. Taylor, *The Sabbatic Question* (Revell), pp. 16, 17.

The first day of the week is mentioned but eight times in the New Testament, six of which are found in the four Gospels, and refer to the day on which Christ arose from the dead. (See Matthew 28:1; Mark 16:2, 9; Luke 24:1; John 20:1, 19.) The other two (Acts 20:7; 1 Corinthians 16:2) refer to the only religious meeting held on the first day of the week after the ascension, in apostolic times, recorded in the New Testament, and to a systematic accounting and laying by in store at home on that day for the poor saints in Judea and Jerusalem.

It is evident, therefore, that the Sabbath of the New Testament is the same as the Sabbath of the Old Testament, and that there is nothing in the New Testament setting aside the seventh-day Sabbath and putting the first day of the week in its place.

Chapter 12

The Good News About
God's Unchangeable Day

The Sabbath and the Law

Of what is the Sabbath commandment a part?

The law of God. (See Exodus 20:8-11.)

What did Christ say of the law?

"Do not think that I came to destroy the Law or the Prophets. I did not come to destroy but to fulfill." Matthew 5:17.

NOTE—"He [Christ] fulfilled the moral law by obeying, by bringing out its fullness of meaning, by showing its intense spirituality, and He established it on a surer basis than ever as the eternal law of righteousness. He fulfilled the ceremonial and typical law, not only by conforming to its requirements, but by realizing its spiritual significance. He filled up the shadowy outlines of the types, and, thus fulfilled, they pass away, and it is no longer necessary for us to observe the Passover or slay the daily lamb: we have the substance in Christ."—*The International Standard Bible Encyclopedia*, vol. 3, p. 1847.

How enduring did He say the law is?

"Till heaven and earth pass away, one jot or one tittle will by no means pass from the law till all is fulfilled." Verse 18.

What did He say of those who break the commandments and teach others to do so?

"Whoever therefore breaks one of the least of these commandments, and teaches men so, shall be called least in the kingdom of heaven; but whoever does and teaches them, *he shall be called great in the kingdom of heaven.*" Verse 19.

NOTE—From this it is evident that all ten commandments are binding in the Christian dispensation, and that Christ had no thought of changing any of them. One of these commands was the observance of the seventh day as the Sabbath. But most Christians keep the first day of the week instead.

"It is a remarkable and regrettable fact that while most Christians regard the Decalogue as a whole as being of personal and perpetual obligation, so many should make the fourth commandment as exception. It is the most complete and comprehensive of them all and, unlike the rest, is expressed both positively and negatively."—W. C. Procter, in *Moody Bible Institute Monthly,* December 1933, p. 160.

Many believe that Christ changed the Sabbath. But from His own words we see that He came for no such purpose. The responsibility for this change must therefore be looked for elsewhere.

Those who believe that Jesus changed the Sabbath base it only on a supposition: "Jesus, after his resurrection, changed the Sabbath from the seventh to the first day of the week; thus showing his authority as Lord even of the Sabbath. . . . *When Jesus gave instructions for this change we are not told,* but very likely during the time when he spoke to his apostles of the things pertaining to his kingdom. Acts 1:3. This is probably one of the many unrecorded things which Jesus did. John 20:30; 21:25."—Amos Binney and Daniel Steele (Methodist), *Binney's Theological Compend Improved,* p. 171. (Italics supplied.)

What kind of worship does the Savior call that which is not according to God's commandments?

"And *in vain they worship Me,* teaching as doctrines the commandments of men." Matthew 15:9.

History of the Sabbath

For how long a time was the seventh-day Sabbath observed in the Christian church?

For many centuries. In fact, its observance has never wholly ceased in the Christian church.

NOTE—Mr. Morer, a learned clergyman of the Church of England, says: "The *Primitive Christians* had a great veneration for the *Sabbath,* and spent the *Day* in Devotion and Sermons. And 'tis not to be doubled but they derived this Practice from the *Apostles* themselves."—*A Discourse in Six Dialogues on the Name, Notion, and Observation of the Lord's Day,* p. 189.

"A history of the problem shows that in some places, it was really only after some centuries that the Sabbath rest really was entirely abolished, and by that time the practice of observing a bodily rest on the Sunday had taken its place."—Vincent J. Kelly, *Forbidden Sunday and Feast-Day Occupations*, p. 15.

Lyman Coleman says: "Down even to the fifth century the observance of the Jewish Sabbath was continued in the Christian church, but with a rigor and a solemnity gradually diminishing until it was wholly discontinued."—*Ancient Christianity Exemplified*, chap. 26, sec. 2.

The church historian Socrates, who wrote in the fifth century, says: "Almost all the churches throughout the world celebrate the sacred mysteries on the Sabbath of every week, yet the Christians of Alexandria and at Rome, on account of some ancient tradition, have ceased to do this."—*Ecclesiastical History*, book 5, chap. 22, in *A Select Library of Nicene and Post-Nicene Fathers*, 2nd series, vol. 2, p. 32.

Sozomen, another historian of the same period, writes: "The people of Constantinople, and almost everywhere, assemble together on the Sabbath, as well as on the first day of the week, which custom is never observed at Rome or at Alexandria."—*Ecclesiastical History*, book 7, chap. 19, in the same volume as the above quotation.

All this would have been inconceivable had there been a divine command given for the change of the Sabbath.

Sunday Observance

How did Sunday observance originate?

As voluntary celebration of the resurrection, a custom without pretense of divine authority.

NOTE—"Opposition to Judaism introduced the particular festival of Sunday very early, indeed, into the place of the Sabbath. . . . The festival of Sunday, like all other festivals, was always only a human ordinance, and it was far from the intentions of the apostles to establish a Divine command in this respect, far from them, and from the early apostolic Church, to transfer the laws of the Sabbath to Sunday. Perhaps at the end of the second century a false application of this kind had begun to take place; for men appear by that time to have considered labouring on Sunday as a sin."—Augustus Neander, *The History of the Christian Religion and Church* (Rose's translation from the first German ed.), p. 186.

"The observance of the Sunday was at first supplemental to that of the Sabbath, but in proportion as the gulf between the Church and the Synagogue widened, the Sabbath became less and less important and ended at length in being entirely neglected."—L. Duchesne, *Christian Worship: Its Origin and Evolution*, from the 4th French ed. by M. L. McClure (London, 1910), p. 47.

Who first enjoined Sundaykeeping by law?

Constantine the Great.

NOTE—"(1) That the Sunday was in the beginning not looked on as a day of bodily repose; nor was an analogy drawn between the Jewish Sabbath and the Christian Sunday, except as days of worship. . . .

"(3) The keeping of the Sunday rest arose from the custom of the people and the constitution of the Church. . . .

"(5) Tertullian was probably the first to refer to a cessation of worldly affairs on the Sunday; the Council of Laodicea issued the first conciliar legislation for that day; Constantine I issued the first civil legislation; St. Martin of Braga was probably the first to use the term 'servile work' in its present theological sense."—Vincent J. Kelly, *Forbidden Sunday and Feast-Day Occupations*, p. 203.

"The earliest recognition of the observance of Sunday as a legal duty is a constitution of Constantine in 321 A.D., enacting that all courts of justice, inhabitants of towns, and workshops were to be at rest on Sunday (*venerabili die solis*), with an exception in favor of those engaged in agricultural labor."—*Encyclopedia Britannica*, 11th ed., art. "Sunday."

"On the venerable Day of the Sun let the magistrates and people residing in cities rest, and let all workshops be closed. In the country, however, persons engaged in agriculture may freely and lawfully continue their pursuits; because it often happens that another day is not so suitable for grain sowing or for vine planting; lest by neglecting the proper moment for such operations the bounty of heaven should be lost. (Given the 7th day of March, Crispus and Constantine being consuls each of them for the second time.)"—*Codex Justinianus*, lib. 3, tit. 12, 3; translated in *History of the Christian Church*, by Philip Schaff, D.D. (Scribners, 1902 ed.), vol. 3, p. 380.

This edict, issued by Constantine, who first opened the way for the union of church and state in the Roman Empire, in a manner supplied the lack of a divine command for Sunday observance. It was one of the important steps in bringing about and establishing the change of the Sabbath.

What does Eusebius say on this subject?

"All things whatsoever that it was duty to do on the Sabbath, these we [the church] have transferred to the Lord's day."—Translated from Eusebius, *Commentary on the Psalm*, in Migne, *Patrologia Graeca*, vol. 23, cols, 1171, 1172.

NOTE—The change of the Sabbath was the result of the combined efforts of church and state, and it took centuries to accomplish it. Eusebius of Caesarea (270-338) was a noted bishop of the church, biographer and flatterer of Constantine, and the reputed father of ecclesiastical history.

By what church council was the observance of the seventh day forbidden and Sunday observance enjoined?

Bible Answers

The Council of Laodicea, in Asia Minor, fourth century.

NOTE—Canon 29 reads: "Christians shall not Judaize and be idle on Saturday [*sabbato*, the Sabbath], but shall work on that day; but the Lord's day they shall especially honour, and, as being Christians, shall, if possible, do no work on that day. If, however, they are found Judaizing, they shall be shut out [*anathema*] from Christ."—Charles Joseph Hefele, *A History of the Councils of the Church* (1896 English ed.), vol. 2, p. 316.

The Puritan William Prynne said (1655) that "the Council of Laodicea . . . first set[t]led the observation of the Lords-day, and prohibited . . . the keeping of the Jewish Sabbath under an Anathema."—*A Brief Polemicall Dissertation Concerning . . . the Lords-day-Sabbath*, p. 44.

What was done at the Council of Laodicea was but one of the steps by which the change of the Sabbath was effected. It was looked back upon as the first church council to forbid Sabbath observance and enjoin Sunday rest as far as possible, but it was not so strict as later decrees. Different writers give conflicting dates for this Council of Laodicea. The exact date is unknown, but may be placed "generally somewhere between the years 343 and 381." (Hefele, vol. 2, p. 298.)

Have church leaders claimed to have changed the Sabbath?

Yes. The Catholic Church has claimed responsibility for this change.

NOTE—The *Catechismus Romanus* was commanded by the Council of Trent and published by the Vatican Press, by order of Pope Pius V, in 1566. This catechism for priests says: "It pleased the church of God, that the religious celebration of the Sabbath day should be transferred to 'the Lord's day.'"—*Catechism of the Council of Trent* (Donovan's translation, 1867), part 3, chap. 4, p. 345. The same, in slightly different wording, is the McHugh and Callan translation (1937 ed.), p. 402.

"The pope is of so great authority and power that he can modify, explain, or interpret even divine laws. . . . The pope can modify divine law, since his power is not of man, but of God, and he acts as vicegerent of God upon the earth."—Translated from Lucius Ferraris, *Prompta Bibliotheca* (Ready Library), "Papa," art. 2.

"*Ques.*—How prove you that the Church hath power to command feasts and holydays?

"*Ans.*—By the very act of changing the Sabbath into Sunday, which Protestants allow of; and therefore they fondly contradict themselves, by keeping Sunday strictly, and breaking most other feasts commanded by the same Church.—Henry Tuberville, *An Abridgment of the Christian Doctrine* (1833 approbation), p. 58. (Same statement in *Manual of Christian Doctrine*, ed. by Daniel Ferris [1916 ed.], p. 67.)

"*Ques.*—Have you any other way of proving that the Church has power to institute festivals of precept?

"*Ans.*—Had she not such power, she could not have done that in which all modern religionists agree with her;—she could not have substituted the observance of Sunday, the first day of the week, for the observance of Saturday, the seventh day, a change for which there is no Scriptural authority.—Stephen Keenan, *A Doctrinal Catechism* (3rd ed.), p. 174.

"The Catholic Church, . . . by virtue of her divine mission, changed the day from Saturday to Sunday."—*The Catholic Mirror*, official organ of Cardinal Gibbons, Sept. 23, 1893.

"1. Is Saturday the 7th day according to the Bible and the 10 Commandments?

"**I answer yes.**

"2. Is Sunday the first day of the week, and did the Church change the 7th day—Saturday—for Sunday, the 1st day?

"**I answer yes.**

"3. Did Christ change the day?

"**I answer no!** Faithfully yours,

"J. Card. Gibbons"—Gibbons' Autograph letter.

"*Ques.*—Which is the Sabbath day?

"*Ans.*—Saturday is the Sabbath day.

"*Ques.*—Why do we observe Sunday instead of Saturday?

"*Ans.*—We observe Sunday instead of Saturday because the Catholic Church transferred the solemnity from Saturday to Sunday."—Peter Geiermann, *The Convert's Catechism of Catholic Doctrine* (1946 ed.), p. 50. Geiermann received the "apostolic blessing" of Pope Pius X on his labors, Jan. 25, 1910.

Do religious authorities acknowledge that there is no command in the Bible for the sanctification of Sunday?

Both Catholic and Protestant authorities acknowledge this fact. First we quote Catholic scholars:

NOTE—"You may read the Bible from Genesis to Revelation, and you will not find a single line authorizing the sanctification of Sunday. The Scriptures enforce the religious observance of Saturday, a day which we never sanctify."—James Cardinal Gibbons, *The Faith of Our Fathers* (1917 ed.), pp. 72, 73.

"Nowhere in the Bible is it stated that worship should be changed from Saturday to Sunday. The fact is that the Church was in existence for several centuries before the Bible was given to the world. The Church made the Bible, the Bible did not make the Church.

"Now the Church . . . instituted, by God's authority, Sunday as the day of worship. This same Church, by the same divine authority, taught the doctrine of Purgatory long before the Bible was made. We have, therefore, the same authority for Purgatory as we have for Sunday."—Martin L. Scott, *Things Catholics Are Asked About* (1927 ed.), p. 136.

"If we consulted the Bible only, we should still have to

keep holy the Sabbath Day, that is, Saturday."—John Laux, *A Course in Religion for Catholic High Schools and Academies* (1936 ed.), vol. 1, p. 51. (Quoted by permission of Benziger Brothers, Inc., proprietors of the copyright.)

"For ages all Christian nations looked to the Catholic Church, and, as we have seen, the various states enforced by law her ordinances as to worship and cessation of Labor on Sunday, Protestantism, in discarding the authority of the church, has no good reason for its Sunday theory, and ought logically, to keep Saturday as the Sabbath.

"The Sunday, as a day of the week set apart for the obligatory public worship of Almighty God, to be sanctified by a suspension of all servile labor, trade, and worldly avocations and by exercises of devotion, *is purely a creation of the Catholic Church.*"—*The American Catholic Quarterly Review,* January 1883, pp. 152, 139. (Italics supplied.)

"If Protestants would follow the Bible, they should worship God on the Sabbath Day. In keeping the Sunday they are following a law of the Catholic Church."—Albert Smith, chancellor of the Archdiocese of Baltimore, replying for the cardinal in a letter of Feb. 10, 1920.

"Some theologians have held that God likewise directly determined the Sunday as the day of worship in the New Law, that He Himself has explicitly substituted the Sunday for the Sabbath. But this theory is now entirely abandoned. It is now commonly held that God simply gave His Church the power to set aside whatever day or days she would deem suitable as Holy Days. The Church chose Sunday, the first day of the week, and in the course of time added other days, as holy days."—Vincent J. Kelly (Catholic), *Forbidden Sunday and Feast-Day Occupations* (1943 ed.), p. 2.

Do Protestant writers agree with this?

They do.

NOTE—"The Lord's day was merely of ecclesiastical institution. It was not introduced by virtue of the fourth commandment."—Jeremy Taylor (Church of England), *Ductor Dubitantium,* part 1, book 2, chap. 2, rule 6, secs. 51, 59 (1850 ed.), vol. 9, pp. 458, 464.

"The Lord's Day is not sanctified by any specific command or by any inevitable inference. In all the New Testament there is no hint or suggestion of a legal obligation binding any man, whether saint or sinner, to observe the Day. Its sanctity arises only out of what it means to the true believer."—J. J. Taylor (Baptist), *The Sabbatic Question,* p. 72.

"Because it was requisite to appoint a certain day, that the people might know when they ought to come together, it appears that the [Christian] Church did for that purpose appoint the Lord's day."—Augsburg Confession, part 2, art. 7, in Philip Schaff, *The Creeds of Christendom* (Harper), vol. 3, p. 69.

"And where are we told in the Scriptures that we are to keep the first day at all? We are commanded to keep the seventh; but we are nowhere commanded to keep the first day. . . . The reason why we keep the first day of the week holy instead of the seventh is for the same reason that we observe many other things, not because the Bible, but because the church, has enjoined it."—Isaac Williams (Anglican), *Plain Sermons on the Catechism,* vol. 1, pp. 334, 336.

"The Christian Church made no formal, but a gradual and almost unconscious, transference of the one day to the other."—F. W. Farrar, *The Voice From Sinai,* p. 167. This of itself is evidence that there was no divine command for the change of the Sabbath.

"They [the Catholics] allege the change of the Sabbath into the Lord's day, contrary, as it seemeth, to the Decalogue; and they have no example more in their mouths than the change of the Sabbath. They will needs have the Church's power to be very great, because it hath dispensed with a precept of the Decalogue."—Augsburg Confession (Lutheran), part 2, art. 7, in Philip Schaff, *The Creeds of Christendom* (Scribners, 4th ed.), vol. 3, p. 64.

"It [the Roman Catholic Church] reversed the Fourth Commandment by doing away with the Sabbath of God's word, and instituting Sunday as a holiday."—N. Summerbell, *History of the Christian Church* (1873), p. 415.

Chapter 13

The Good News About
God's Everlasting Grace

The Purpose of the Law

What is the purpose of the law?

"Therefore by the deeds of the law no flesh will be justified in His sight, for *by the law is the knowledge of sin.*" Romans 3:20.

How particular is God concerning Christian conduct?

"For whoever shall keep the whole law, and yet stumble in one point, he is guilty of all." James 2:10.

Christ Saves Humanity, Magnifies Law

What is the gospel declared to be?

"I am not ashamed of the gospel of Christ, for it is *the power of God to salvation for everyone who believes.*" Romans 1:16.

What is the significance of the name Jesus?

"You shall call His name Jesus, for *He will save His people from their sins.*" Matthew 1:21.

In whom is this power to save from sin revealed?

"But we preach . . . *Christ the power of God* and the wisdom of God." 1 Corinthians 1:23, 24.

How was Christ's attitude toward God's law foretold?

"*I delight to do Your will, O my God, and Your law is within my heart.*" Psalm 40:8.

What does Christ promise of the new covenant?

"But now He has obtained a more excellent ministry, inasmuch as He is also *Mediator* of a better covenant." "For this is the covenant that I will make with the house of Israel after those days, says the Lord: *I will put My laws in their mind and write them on their hearts.*" Hebrews 8:6, 10.

What must we do in order to benefit by Christ's work?

"For with the heart one *believes* unto righteousness, and with the mouth *confession* is made unto salvation." Romans 10:10.

For what did the apostle Paul trust Christ?

"I also count all things loss . . . that I may gain Christ and be found in Him, not having my own righteousness, which is from the law, but that which is through faith in Christ, *the righteousness which is from God by faith.*" Philippians 3:8, 9.

Does the faith that brings righteousness abolish the law?

"Do we then make void the law through faith? Certainly not! On the contrary, *we establish the law.*" Romans 3:31.

NOTE—In the gospel, the law, first written in the heart of Christ, becomes "the law of the Spirit of life in Christ Jesus," and is thus transferred to the heart of the believer, where Christ dwells by faith. Thus the new covenant promise is fulfilled. This is righteousness by faith—a righteousness that is witnessed by the law, and revealed in the life in harmony with the law. Such faith, instead of making void the law, establishes it in the heart of the believer.

"The law demands obedience, but cannot produce it; it is holy in itself, but it cannot make us holy; it convinces of sin, but it cannot cure it; it reveals the disease, but it cannot provide the remedy; while the gospel both requires and enables, saves and sanctifies (Rom. 3:19-22; 4:15; 5:20, 21; 7:7-13; 2 Cor. 3:7-9; Gal. 3:21-24; 1 Tim. 1:8-11). . . .

"While it is in the very nature of all law to provoke opposition to itself in our wayward minds and willful hearts, it is the essence of the gospel to appeal to the two strongest motives that actuate men and women—gratitude and love (contrast Rom. 7:5, 7-11; with 6:1-15; 2 Cor. 5:14, 15). . . .

"The gospel shows us the Saviour whom we need, and declares that he has fully obeyed the precepts of the law by his apostles life as our great representative, as well as completely exhausted its penalties through his atoning death as our great substitute (2 Cor. 5:21). . . . Divine justice and righteousness have been more entirely vindicated through his work for men than they could have been by the obedience or sufferings of the whole human race!

"It is the aim alike of the law and of the gospel to secure obedience, but the law compels us to it as a duty, making it irksome and distasteful, while the gospel constrains us to it as a privilege, rendering it easy and delightful. The law sets obedience before us as a means of salvation, and makes blessing strictly conditional upon it. The gospel reveals it as the natural consequence of redemption, and enjoins obedience as the necessary result of blessing."—William C. Procter, *Moody Bible Institute Monthly* (copyrighted), November 1933, pp. 107, 108. Used by permission.

What did Christ take away?

"Behold! The Lamb of God who takes away *the sin of the world!*" John 1:29.

What has Christ abolished?

"Jesus Christ, who has *abolished death* and brought life and immortality to light through the gospel." 2 Timothy 1:10.

NOTE—"Man . . . needs to be solemnly reminded that the law of the spirit of life in Christ sets him free from *the law of sin and death,* but not from the law of God."—G. Campbell Morgan, *The Ten Commandments* (Revell, 1901 ed.), p. 12.

What change is brought about through the gospel?

"But we all, with unveiled face, beholding as in a mirror the glory of the Lord, are being *transformed into the same image* from glory to glory, just as by the Spirit of the Lord." 2 Corinthians 3:18.

NOTE—It is sometimes claimed that Christ changed, abolished, or took away the law, and put the gospel in its place; but this shows a misapprehension of the real work of Christ. The individual believer is changed by beholding the glory revealed in the gospel (2 Corinthians 4:4; John 1:14); death has been abolished through the death of Christ; and sin has been taken away by the great Sin Bearer, but the law of God still remains unchanged as the very foundation of His throne.

What spiritual interpretation did Christ give to the sixth and seventh commandments?

"You have heard that it was said to those of old, 'You shall not murder, and whoever murders will be in danger of the judgment.' But I say to you that *whoever is angry with his brother* without a cause shall be in danger of the judgment." Matthew 5:21, 22. "You have heard that it was said to those of old, 'You shall not commit adultery.' But I say to you that *whoever looks at a woman to lust for her has already committed adultery with her in his heart.*" Verses 27, 28.

Of what prophecy was this teaching a fulfillment?

"The Lord is well pleased for His righteousness' sake; *He will exalt the law and make it honorable.*" Isaiah 42:21.

NOTE—Christ not only gave a spiritual interpretation to the law, and thus observed it, but He showed the holiness and the immutable nature of the law by dying on the cross to pay the penalty of its transgression. In this way, above all, He magnified the law.

Grace and the Law

In what promise was the gospel preached to Abraham?

"And the Scripture . . . preached the gospel to Abraham beforehand, saying, '*In you all the nations shall be blessed.*'" Galatians 3:8.

On what basis was Abraham accounted righteous?

"For what does the Scripture say? '*Abraham believed God, and it was accounted to him for righteousness.*'" Romans 4:3.

What scripture cuts off all hope of justification by works?

"Therefore *by the deeds of the law no flesh will be justified in His sight,* for by the law is the knowledge of sin." Romans 3:20.

In what way are all believers in Jesus justified?

"Being *justified freely by His grace* through the redemption that is in Christ Jesus." Verse 24.

Is the believer expected to go on in sin after this?

"What shall we say then? Shall we continue in sin that grace may abound? Certainly not! How shall we who died to sin live any longer in it?" Romans 6:1, 2.

What was Christ's personal attitude toward the law?

"Do not think that I came to destroy the Law or the Prophets. *I did not come to destroy but to fulfill.*" Matthew 5:17. "If you keep My commandments, you will abide in My love, just as *I have kept My Father's commandments* and abide in His love." John 15:10.

What scripture shows that God's remnant people will understand the proper relation between law and gospel?

"Here is the patience of the saints; *here are those who keep the commandments of God and the faith of Jesus.*" Revelation 14:12.

NOTE—"God has not left men enmeshed in their own disobedience—he has provided a way of restoration. This is not by pulling the heavenly standard down to the level of our guiltiness and weakness, but by lifting men up to the level of the eternal standard of his holiness. . . . This restoration is *restoration to a state of obedience to the Law.* . . . The atonement of Jesus Christ . . . bears an eternal relation to the Law of God, the Law which is holy, just and good. . . . [As the believer is] delivered by the work of Christ from the penalty of a broken law, and given a new heart by the Holy Spirit, by which he loves the way of obedience that once he shunned, the Law and the gospel are seen working in glorious harmony for the blessing of the redeemed man. To achieve this is *the one great purpose* of the proclamation of the gospel."—O.C.S. Wallace, *What Baptists Believe,* pp. 83, 84. (Italics supplied.) Copyright 1934 by the Sunday School Board of the Southern Baptist Convention. Used by permission.

Chapter 14

The Good News About
Baptism

Belief, Repentance, and Baptism

What ordinance is closely associated with believing the gospel?

"And He said to them, 'Go into all the world and preach the gospel to every creature. He who believes and is *baptized* will be saved; but he who does not believe will be condemned.'" Mark 16:15, 16.

What did the apostle Peter associate with baptism in his instruction on the day of Pentecost?

"Then Peter said to them, *'Repent,* and let every one of you be baptized in the name of Jesus Christ for the remission of sins.'" Acts 2:38.

In reply to his inquiry concerning salvation, what was the Philippian jailer told to do?

"So they said, *'Believe on the Lord Jesus Christ,* and you will be saved, you and your household.'" Acts 16:31.

What followed immediately after the jailer and his family had accepted Christ as their Savior?

"And he took them [Paul and Silas] the same hour of the night and washed their stripes. And immediately he and all his family were *baptized.*" Verse 33.

Spiritual Significance of Baptism

In connection with Christian baptism, what is washed away?

"And now why are you waiting? Arise and be baptized, and *wash away your sins,* calling on the name of the Lord." Acts 22:16. (See Titus 3:5; 1 Peter 3:21.)

By what means are sins washed away?

"To Him who loved us and washed us from our sins *in His own blood.*" Revelation 1:5.

Union With Christ in Baptism

In whose name are believers to be baptized?

"Go therefore and make disciples of all the nations, baptizing them in the name of the *Father* and of the *Son* and of the *Holy Spirit.*" Matthew 28:19.

When believers are baptized into Christ, whom do they put on?

"For as many of you as were baptized into Christ have *put on Christ.*" Galatians 3:27.

Into what experience are those baptized who are baptized into Christ?

"Or do you not know that as many of us as were baptized into Christ Jesus were *baptized into His death?*" Romans 6:3.

NOTE—Baptism is a gospel ordinance commemorating the *death, burial, and resurrection* of Christ. In baptism public testimony is given to the effect that the one baptized has been crucified with Christ, buried with Him, and is raised with Him to walk in newness of life. Only one mode of baptism can rightly represent these facts of experience, and that is immersion—the mode followed by Christ and the primitive church.

How is such a baptism described?

"Therefore we were *buried with Him* through baptism into death, that just as Christ was raised from the dead by the glory of the Father, even so we also should walk in newness of life." Verse 4.

How fully are we thus united with Christ in His experience of death and resurrection?

"For if we have been *united together* in the likeness of His *death,* certainly we also shall be in the likeness of *His resurrection.*" Verse 5.

What will follow this union with Christ?

"Now if we died with Christ, we believe that we shall also *live with Him.*" Verse 8.

In what working of God is faith to be exercised in connection with baptism?

"Buried with Him in baptism, in which you also were raised with Him *through faith in the working of God, who raised Him from the dead.*" Colossians 2:12.

Bible Answers

Baptism and the Holy Spirit

At the beginning of His ministry, what example did Jesus set for the benefit of His followers?

"Then Jesus came from Galilee to John at the Jordan to be *baptized* by him." Matthew 3:13.

What occurred at the baptism of Jesus?

"When He had been baptized, Jesus came up immediately from the water; and behold, the heavens were opened to Him, and *He saw the Spirit of God descending like a dove and alighting upon Him.* And suddenly a voice came from heaven, saying, *'This is My beloved Son, in whom I am well pleased.'*" Verses 16, 17.

What promise is made to those who repent and are baptized?

"Then Peter said to them, "Repent, and let every one of you be baptized in the name of Jesus Christ for the remission of sins; and you *shall receive the gift of the Holy Spirit.*'" Acts 2:38.

What instruction did the apostle Peter give concerning the Gentiles who had believed?

"'Can anyone forbid water, that these should not be baptized who have received the Holy Spirit just as we have?' *And he commanded them to be baptized in the name of the Lord.*" Acts 10:47, 48.

Philip Baptizes an Ethiopian and Samaritans

What question did the eunuch ask after Philip had preached Jesus unto him?

"Now as they went down the road, they came to some water. And the eunuch said, 'See, here is water. *What hinders me from being baptized?'*" Acts 8:36.

Where did Philip go to baptize the eunuch?

"So he commanded the chariot to stand still. And both Philip and the eunuch *went down into the water,* and he baptized him." Verse 38.

How did the people of Samaria publicly testify to their faith in the preaching of Philip?

"But when they believed Philip as he preached the things concerning the kingdom of God and the name of Jesus Christ, both men and women *were baptized.*" Verse 12.

Unity and Heavenly Purpose

How perfect is the unity into which believers are brought by being baptized into Christ?

"For as the body is one and has many members, but all the members of that one body, being many, are one body, so also is Christ. For by one Spirit we were all *baptized into one body*—whether Jews or Greeks, whether slaves or free—and have all been *made to drink into one Spirit.*" 1 Corinthians 12:12, 13.

After being united with Christ in the likeness of His death and resurrection, what should the believer do?

"If then you were raised with Christ, *seek those things which are above,* where Christ is, sitting at the right hand of God." Colossians 3:1.

Chapter 15

The Good News About
Death

Of what were humans formed in the beginning?

"And the Lord God formed man *of the dust of the ground*." Genesis 2:7.

What act made a human being a living soul?

"And the Lord God . . . *breathed into his nostrils the breath of life;* and man became a living being." Verse 7.

NOTE—The living soul was not put *into* the human; but the breath of *life* that was put into a human made *that human*—formed of the earth—a *living* soul, or creature. "Man became a living being," says the Smith-Goodspeed American translation. (University of Chicago Press.)

The Hebrew original translated "living soul" in this text is *nephesh chaiyah,* the same expression used in Genesis 1:24, translated "living creature."

The word *nephesh* occurs more than 700 times in the Hebrew Old Testament. In the King James Version the word is translated:

- 428 times as "soul." For example: Genesis 2:7; 12:5; Numbers 9:13; Psalm 6:3; Isaiah 1:14.
- 119 times, "life" (life's, lives). For example: Genesis 1:20, 30; 9:4; 1 Kings 19:14; Job 6:11; Psalm 38:12.
- 29 times, "person." For example: Numbers 31:19; 35:11, 15, 30; Deuteronomy 27:25; Joshua 20:3, 9; 1 Samuel 22:22.
- 15 times, "mind." For example: Deuteronomy 18:6; Jeremiah 15:1.
- 15 times, "heart." For example: Exodus 23:9; Proverbs 23:7.
- 9 times, "creature." Genesis 1:21, 24; 2:19; 9:10, 12, 15, 16; Leviticus 11:46.
- 7 times, "body" (or dead body). Leviticus 21:11; Numbers 6:6; 9:6, 7, 10; 19:13; Haggai 2:13.
- 5 times, "dead." Leviticus 19:28; 21:1; 22:4; Number 5:2; 6:11.
- 3 times, "man." Exodus 12:16; 2 Kings 12:4; 1 Chronicles 5:21.
- 3 times, "me." Numbers 23:10; Judges 16:30; 1 Kings 20:32.
- 3 times, "beast." Leviticus 24:18.
- 2 times, "ghost." Job 11:20; Jeremiah 15:9.
- 1 time, "fish." Isaiah 19:10.

One or more times as various forms of the personal pronouns. (These figures are from Young's *Analytical Concordance.*)

Are other creatures besides humans called "living souls"?

"So God created great sea creatures and every living thing that moves, with which the waters abounded, according to their kind, and every winged bird according to its kind. And God saw that it was good." Genesis 1:21. "Out of the ground the Lord God formed every beast of the field and every bird of the air, and brought them to Adam to see what he would call them. And whatever Adam called each living creature, that was its name." Genesis 2:19.

NOTE—Look up the nine instances of *nephesh,* "soul," translated as "creature" in the King James Version, and you will see that they all refer to animals as "living creatures," or, as the words might have been translated, "living souls." On the phrase *nephesh chaiyah,* living soul or creature, in Genesis 1:24, Adam Clarke says: "A general term to express all creatures endued with animal life, in any of its infinitely varied gradations, from the half-reasoning elephant down to the stupid potto, or lower still, to the polype, which seems equally to share the vegetable and animal life."

An examination of the various occurrences of *nephesh* in the Old Testament shows that *nephesh* describes the individual rather than being a constituent part of the individual. It would be more correct, therefore, to say that a human *is* as *nephesh,* or "soul," than that a human *has* a *nephesh,* or "soul." True, the expressions "my soul," "thy soul," "his soul," etc., occur frequently, but in most instances these are simply idiomatic expressions meaning "myself," "thyself," "himself," etc. Translators recognizing this have at times substituted the personal pronoun. For examples, see Psalm 35:25; Proverbs 6:16; 16:26; Isaiah 5:14. In other instances *nephesh* means "life." Where such is its meaning, "my soul" would mean "my life," "thy life," etc. See 2 Samuel 1:9; Jeremiah 4:30; etc.

In the New Testament the word translated "soul" is the Greek *psuchē.* This is the word that in the Septuagint, the Greek translation of the Hebrew Old Testament, translates the Hebrew word *nephesh.* New Testament writers used *psuchē* as the equivalent of *nephesh,* and did not attach to *psuchē* the pagan Greek concept of the allegedly immortal part of human beings as opposed to the body or perishable part. *Psuchē* is rendered by the following words in the King James Version:

- 58 times, "soul."
- 40 times, "life." For example: Mark 3:4; 10:45; Luke 6:9; 9:56; John 13:37; Romans 11:3; Revelation 8:9; 12:11.
- 3 times, "mind." Acts 14:2; Philippians 1:27; Hebrews 12:3.
- 1 time, "heart." Ephesians 6:6.
- 1 time, "heartily" (literally, "from the soul"). Colossians 3:23.

Psuchē is also used once in John 10:24 and in 2 Corinthians 12:15, in idiomatic phrases that are properly translated by the personal pronoun.

Do others besides humans have the "breath of life"?

"And all flesh died that moved on the earth: *birds* and *cattle* and *beasts* and *every creeping thing* that creeps on the earth, and every man. *All in whose nostrils was the breath of the spirit of life,* all that was on the dry land, died." Genesis 7:21, 22.

When humans give up this spirit, what becomes of it?

"Then the dust will return to the earth as it was, and *the spirit will return to God who gave it.*" Ecclesiastes 12:7.

NOTE—The word translated "breath" is *ruach,* which is defined in Gesenius' Lexicon as *"Rauch:*

"(1) Spirit, breath. *(a)* Breath of the mouth. . . . Hence used of anything quickly perishing. . . . Often used of the vital spirit. . . . *(b)* Breath of the nostrils, snuffing, snoring. . . . Hence anger. . . . *(c)* Breath of air, air in motion, i.e., breeze. . . .

"(2) *Psuche anima,* breath, life, the vital principle, which shows itself in the breathing of the mouth and nostrils (see No. 1, *a, b*), whether of men or of beast, Ecclesiastes 3:21; 8:8; 12:7; . . .

"(3) The rational mind of spirit, *(a)* As the seat of the senses, affections, and emotions of various kinds. . . . *(b)* As to the mode of thinking and acting. . . . *(c)* Of will and counsel. . . . More rarely *(d)* it is applied to the intellect. . . .

"(4) The Spirit of God."—Tregelles' translation (1875 ed.).

The word "spirit" in the Old Testament is always from *ruach,* except twice (Job 26:4 and Proverbs 20:27 from *neshamah*). *Ruach,* besides being rendered 232 times as "spirit," is also translated:

- 90 times, "wind." ("Wind" in the Old Testament is always a translation of *ruach.*)
- 28 times, "breath." For example: Genesis 6:17; 7:15, 22; Job 12:10; Psalms 104:29; 146:4; Ecclesiastes 3:19.
- 8 times, "mind." Genesis 26:35; Proverbs 29:11; Ezekiel 11:5; 20:32; Daniel 5:20; Habakkuk 1:11.

- 4 times, "blast." Exodus 15:8; 2 Kings 19:7; Isaiah 25:4; 37:7.

Also translated one or more times by the following words: "anger," "air," "tempest," "vain."

At death the spirit goes back to the great Author of life. Having come from Him, it belongs to God, and humans can have it eternally only as a gift from God, through Jesus Christ. (Romans 6:23.) When the spirit goes back to God, the dust, from which the body is formed, goes back *as it was,* to the earth, and the individual no longer exists as a living, conscious, thinking being.

"Our personal identity is preserved in the resurrection, though not the same particles of matter or material substance as went into the grave. The wondrous works of God are a mystery to man. The spirit, the character of man, is returned to God, there to be preserved. In the resurrection every man will have his own character. God in His own time will call forth the dead, giving again the breath of life, and bidding the dry bones live. The same form will come forth, but it will be free of disease and every defect. It lives again bearing the same individuality of features, so that friend will recognize friend. There is no law of God in nature which shows that God gives back the same identical particles of matter which composed the body before death. God shall give the righteous dead a body that will please Him."—E. G. White, in *The SDA Bible Commentary,* vol. 6, p. 1093.

From Wrath and Death to Life

Who only have hold of the life eternal?

"He who has the Son has life; he who does not have the Son of God does not have life." 1 John 5:12.

NOTE—The veriest sinners have this temporal life; but when they yield up this life, they have no prospect or promise of the life eternal. That can be received only through Christ.

Why was Adam driven from Eden and the tree of life?

"And now, lest he put out his hand and take also of the tree of life, and eat, and *live forever."* Genesis 3:22.

What was done to keep human beings away from the tree of life?

"So He drove out the man; and He placed cherubim at the east of the garden of Eden, and a flaming sword which turned every way, to guard the way to the tree of life." Verse 24.

How are all individuals in the natural state regarded?

"Among whom also we all once conducted ourselves in the lusts of our flesh, fulfilling the desires of the flesh and of the mind, and were by nature *children of wrath,* just as the others." Ephesians 2:3.

If the wrath of God abides on us, of what are we deprived?

"He who believes in the Son has everlasting life; and he who does not believe the Son *shall not see life,* but the wrath of God abides on him." John 3:36.

Through whom can we be saved from wrath and given immortality?

"Much more then, having now been justified by His blood, we shall be saved from wrath through Him." Romans 5:9. "*Our Savior Jesus Christ, who has abolished death and brought life and immortality to light through the gospel.*" 2 Timothy 1:10.

Who only possesses inherent immortality?

"The blessed and only Potentate, the King of kings and Lord of lords, *who alone has immortality.*" 1 Timothy 6:15, 16.

NOTE—This word for immortality as applied to God is not *aphtharsia,* "incorruptibility," which is used twice, 2 Timothy 1:10 and Romans 2:7, but *athanasia,* "deathlessness," which is used also in 1 Corinthians 15:53, 54. God is the only being who possesses original life or immortality in Himself. All others must receive it from God. (See John 5:26; 6:27; 10:10, 27, 28; Romans 6:23; 1 John 5:11.)

To whom is eternal life promised?

"Eternal life to those who by patient continuance in doing good *seek for glory, honor, and immortality.*" Romans 2:7.

NOTE—We do not need to seek for a thing that we already possess. The fact that we are to seek for immortality is proof in itself that we do not now possess it.

Again, it would mar the felicity of our employment in heaven could we look upon earth and see our friends and relatives suffering from persecution, want, cold, or hunger, or sorrowing for the dead. God's way is best—that all sentient life, animation, activity, thought, and consciousness should cease at death, and all should wait till the resurrection for their eternal reward. (See Hebrews 11:39, 40.)

When will the faithful be changed to immortality?

"We shall not all sleep, but *we shall all be changed*—in a moment, in the twinkling of an eye, *at the last trumpet.* For the trumpet will sound, and the dead will be raised incorruptible, and we shall be changed." 1 Corinthians 15:51, 52.

What is then to be swallowed up?

"So when this corruptible has put on incorruption, and this mortal has put on immortality, then shall be brought to pass the saying that is written: '*Death is swallowed up in victory.*'" Verse 54. (See verse 57.)

NOTE—Isaiah 25:8 says, "He will swallow up death forever, and the Lord God will wipe away tears from all faces; the rebuke of His people He will take away from all the earth; for the Lord has spoken." When Christ comes in the clouds of heaven, the amazing transformation from mortal to immortal takes place, both of the righteous dead and the righteous living. Then regenerated humanity is completely saved beyond all possibilities of death and will be no longer troubled with this great enemy.

What is the wages of sin?

"For the wages of sin is *death.*" Romans 6:23.

Through whom only is there salvation from sin?

"*Nor is there salvation in any other,* for there is no other name under heaven given among men by which we must be saved." Acts 4:12.

Why did God give His only-begotten Son?

"That whoever believes in Him should not *perish* but have *everlasting life.*" John 3:16.

What does Christ declare Himself to be?

"I am the way, the truth, and *the life.*" John 14:6.

What does He give to those who follow Him?

"My sheep hear My voice, and I know them, and they follow Me. And *I give them eternal life,* and they shall never perish; neither shall anyone snatch them out of My hand." John 10:27, 28.

To whom is the life eternal?

"And this is the testimony: that God has given us eternal life, *and this life is in His Son.*" 1 John 5:11.

Who only have this life?

"*He who has the Son has life;* he who does not have the Son of God does not have life." Verse 12. "Most assuredly, I say to you, *he who hears My word and believes in Him who sent Me has everlasting life,* and shall not come into judgment, but has passed from death into life." John 5:24.

What Death Is Like

By what figure does the Bible represent death?

"But I do not want you to be ignorant, brethren, concerning those who have fallen *asleep,* lest you sorrow as others who have no hope." 1 Thessalonians 4:13. (See also 1 Corinthians 15:18, 20; John 11:11-14.)

NOTE—During sound sleep one is wholly lost to

consciousness; time goes by unmeasured; and mental activity is suspended for the time being.

Where does Daniel represent the dead as sleeping?

"And many of those who *sleep in the dust of the earth* shall awake." Daniel 12:2. (See also Ecclesiastes 3:20; 9:10.)

What does one in this condition know about one's family?

"His sons come to honor, and *he does not know it;* they are brought low, and *he does not perceive it.*" Job 14:21.

What becomes of a person's thoughts at death?

"His spirit departs, he returns to his earth; *in that very day his plans perish.*" Psalm 146:4.

Do the dead know "anything"?

"For the living know that they will die; but *the dead know nothing.*" Ecclesiastes 9:5.

Do they take any part in earthly things?

"Also their love, their hatred, and their envy have now *perished; nevermore will they have a share in anything done under the sun.*" Verse 6.

NOTE—If we remained conscious after death, we would know of the promotion or dishonor of our children; but in death we lose all the attributes of mind—love, hatred, envy, etc. Thus it is plain that our thoughts have perished, and that we can have nothing more to do with the things of this world. But if, as taught by some, our powers of thought continue after death, we live; and if we live, we must be somewhere. Where are we? Are we in heaven, or in hell? If we go to either place at death, what then is the need of a future judgment, or of a resurrection, or of the second coming of Christ? If we go to our reward at death, before the judgment takes place, then our rewards precede our awards.

How much does one know of God when dead?

"For in death *there is no remembrance of You.*" Psalm 6:5.

NOTE—As already seen, the Bible everywhere represents the dead as *asleep,* with not even a remembrance of God. If the dead were in heaven or hell, would Jesus have said, "Our friend Lazarus *sleeps*"? John 11:11. If so, calling him to life was really robbing him of the bliss of heaven that rightly belonged to him. The parable of the rich man and Lazarus (Luke 16) teaches not consciousness in death, but that riches will avail nothing in the judgment and that poverty will not keep one out of heaven.

Where Are the Dead?

Are not the righteous dead in heaven praising God?

"For *David did not ascend into the heavens*" Acts 2:34. *"The dead do not praise the Lord,* nor any who go down into silence." Psalm 115:17.

Where did Job say he would await his final change?

"If a man dies, shall he live again? All the days of my hard service I will wait, *till my change* comes." Job 14:14. *"If I wait for the grave as my house,* if I make my bed in the darkness." Job 17:13.

NOTE—The original Hebrew word for "grave" in this verse is *she'ol,* meaning among other things a dark, hollow, subterranean place, used simply in reference to the abode of the dead in general, without distinguishing between the good and the bad. *(*Young's *Analytical Concordance.)*

The same word is also translated "pit" three times (Numbers 16:30, 33; Job 17:16), and "hell" 31 times (every occurrence of the word "hell" in the Authorized Version of the Old Testament). The translation of *she'ol* as "grave" 31 times bears witness to the unsuitability of the present English word "hell" to the idea of *she'ol,* especially in reference to Jacob (Genesis 37:35; 42:38), Job (Job 14:13), David (Psalm 30:3), and even Christ (Psalm 16:10; cf. Acts 2:27, 31). The American Revised Version avoids choosing between "hell" and "grave" by retaining *she'ol* as an untranslated place name, just as it does the corresponding Greek word *hadēs* in the New Testament. It should be remembered that "hell" in the Old Testament always means *she'ol,* a place of darkness and silence, not a place of fiery torment.

When the Dead Rise Again

What must take place before the dead can praise God?

"Your dead shall live; together with my dead body they shall arise. *Awake and sing, you who dwell in dust;* for . . . the earth shall cast out the dead." Isaiah 26:19.

When did the psalmist say he would be satisfied?

"As for me, I will see Your face in righteousness; I shall be satisfied *when I awake in Your likeness.*" Psalm 17:15.

Were there to be no resurrection of the dead, what would be the condition of those fallen asleep in Christ?

"For if the dead do not rise, then Christ is not risen. . . . *Then also those who have fallen asleep in Christ have perished.*" 1 Corinthians 15:16-18.

When will be the resurrection of the righteous?

"For the Lord Himself will descend from heaven with a shout, with the voice of an archangel, and with the trumpet of God. *And the dead in Christ will rise first."* 1 Thessalonians 4:16.

NOTE—If, as stated in Ecclesiastes 9:5, the dead know not anything, then they have no knowledge of the lapse of time; it will seem to them when they awake that absolutely no time has elapsed. Thousands of years in the grave is, to a dead person, no more than a wink of the eye to the living. And herein lies a most comforting thought in the Bible doctrine of the sleep of the dead. To those who sleep in Jesus, their sleep, whether one year, 1,000 years, or 6,000 years, will be but as if the moment of sad parting were followed instantly by the glad reunion in the presence of Jesus at His glorious appearing and the resurrection of the just.

It ought also to be a comforting thought to those whose lives have been filled with anxiety and grief for deceased loved ones who persisted in sin, to know that they are not now suffering in torment, but, with all the rest of the dead, are quietly sleeping in their graves.

Chapter 16

The Good News About
Hell

What question does the apostle Peter ask regarding the wicked?

"What will be the end of those who do not obey the gospel of God?" 1 Peter 4:17.

What does the Bible say is the wages of sin? What is to be the fate of one who persists in sin?

"For *the wages of sin is death.*" Romans 6:23. "The soul who sins shall *die.*" Ezekiel 18:4.

Completeness of the Destruction

What will be the character of this death?

"These shall be punished with *everlasting destruction.*" 2 Thessalonians 1:9.

What will befall those who do not repent?

"Unless you repent you will all likewise *perish.*" Luke 13:3. "But these, like natural brute beasts made to be caught and destroyed, speak evil of the things they do not understand, and *will utterly perish in their own corruption.*" 2 Peter 2:12.

How does John the Baptist describe the destruction of the wicked?

"He will . . . gather His wheat into the barn; but *He will burn up the chaff with unquenchable fire.*" Matthew 3:12.

For whom was this fire originally prepared?

"Then He will also say to those on the left hand, 'Depart from Me, you cursed, into the everlasting fire *prepared for the devil and his angels.*'" Matthew 25:41.

NOTE—This fire is called "everlasting" (Greek, *aionion*, "age lasting") because of the character of the work it does; just as it is called "unquenchable" (Greek, *asbestos*, "unquenchable," "unquenched") because it cannot be put out, not because it will not go out when it has done its work. "Eternal fire" reduced Sodom and Gomorrah to ashes. (Jude 7; 2 Peter 2:6.)

Will any part of the wicked be left?

"'For behold, the day is coming, burning like an oven, and all the proud, yes, *all* who do wickedly will be stubble. And the day which is coming shall *burn them up,*' says the Lord of hosts, *'that will leave them neither root nor branch.*'" Malachi 4:1.

How completely will human beings be destroyed in hell?

"Fear Him who is able to *destroy both soul and body in hell.*" Matthew 10:28.

NOTE—This scripture proves that the soul is neither immortal nor indestructible.

The everlasting punishment—"destruction"—of the wicked is this destruction of soul and body in hell (Greek, *Geenna* [Gehenna]).

"Hell" in the New Testament is translated from three Greek words:

- *Hadēs*, 10 times. Matthew 11:23; 16:18; Luke 10:15; 16:23; Acts 2:27, 31; Revelation 1:18; 6:8; 20:13, 14. (*Hadēs* is also "grave" once, 1 Corinthians 15:55.)
- *Geenna* (Gehenna), 12 times. Matthew 5:22, 29, 30; 10:28; 18:9; 23:15, 33; Mark 9:43, 45, 47; Luke 12:5; James 3:6.
- *Tartaroō*, 1 time (the only occurrence in the Bible). 2 Peter 2:4.

Hadēs (the lower world, place of the dead, the grave) is the equivalent of *she'ol*. It is used in Acts 2:27, 31, to translate from Psalm 16:10. *Tartaroō*, describing the fall of Satan's rebel angels, is a verb, meaning "to cast down to Tartarus." This is a striking figure of speech, alluding to the Tartarus of Greek mythology, an abyss deeper than Hades, the prison of the Titans, who fought against the gods.

Gehenna, the only other word for hell, is the Valley of Hinnom, used symbolically of the fires of the last great day of judgment. This is the word that is used in Matthew 10:28 to describe the place where the wicked will be destroyed body and soul.

Where, When, and How

When will the wicked be punished?

"But the heavens and the earth which are now preserved by the same word, are *reserved for fire until the day of judgment and perdition of ungodly men.*" 2 Peter 3:7.

NOTE—The present heavens and earth and sinners await the fires of the last day. The Greek for "perdition" is *apoleia*, "loss," "destruction."

What will be the result of the fires of the last day?

"What manner of persons ought you to be . . . , looking for and hastening the coming of the day of God, because of which *the heavens will be dissolved, being on fire, and the elements will melt with fervent heat?*" "Both *the earth and the works that are in it will be burned up.*" Verses 12, 10.

How does Christ say sin and sinners will be eliminated?

"His angels . . . *will gather out of His kingdom all things that offend, and those who practice lawlessness, and will cast them into the furnace of fire.*" Matthew 13:41, 42.

When are the wicked dead to be raised to receive this final punishment?

"But the rest of the dead did not live again *until the thousand years were finished.*" Revelation 20:5.

Whence will come the fire that will destroy them?

"They went up on the breadth of the earth and surrounded the camp of the saints and the beloved city. *And fire came down from God out of heaven and devoured them.*" Verse 9.

NOTE—This is called God's "unusual act"—the work of destruction. (Isaiah 28:21.) But by this means God will once and forever cleanse the universe of sin and all its sad results. Death itself will then be at an end—cast into the lake of fire. (Revelation 20:14.)

By what figure does Malachi describe the destruction of the wicked?

"You shall trample the wicked, for they shall be ashes under the soles of your feet." Malachi 4:3.

NOTE—The wicked are to be utterly destroyed—consumed away into smoke, brought to ashes. Through sin they have forfeited the right to life and an immortal existence, and chosen the way of death and destruction. By their choice they have proved themselves worthless, like chaff, briers, thorns, etc. They will themselves have lost their opportunity to obtain eternal life, by the way in which they used their probationary time. Their destruction will, in fact, be an act of love and mercy on the part of God, for to perpetuate their lives would only be to perpetuate sin, sorrow, suffering, and misery. Terrible, therefore, as this judgment will be, there will, in consequence of it, be nothing of value lost—nothing lost worth saving. The experience of sin will be over, and God's original plan of peopling the earth with a race of holy, happy beings will be carried out. (2 Peter 3:13.)

What is this final destruction of the wicked called?

"This *is the second death.*" Revelation 20:14.

After the burning day, what will appear?

"We, according to His promise, look for *new heavens and a new earth* in which righteousness dwells." 2 Peter 3:13.

How will the righteous be recompensed in the earth?

"Blessed are the meek, for *they shall inherit the earth.*" Matthew 5:5. "Then the righteous will shine forth as the sun *in the kingdom of their Father.*" Matthew 13:43.

NOTE—Satan and the wicked now have this world as their "place." In due time Christ will have it. He will cleanse it from sin and sinners, and restore it, that He may give it to the saints of the Most High for an everlasting possession. (See Daniel 7:18, 22, 27.)

Chapter 17

The Good News About
A Thousand Years of Peace

The Millennium and Judgment

What text definitely brings the millennium to view?

"And I saw thrones, and they sat on them, and *judgment was committed to them.* . . . And *they lived and reigned with Christ for a thousand years.*" Revelation 20:4.

Whom does Paul say the saints are to judge?

"Dare any of you, having a matter against another, go to law before the unrighteous, and not before the saints? Do you not know that the saints will judge the world? . . . *Do you not know that we shall judge angels?*" 1 Corinthians 6:1-3.

NOTE—From these scriptures it is plain that the saints of all ages are to be engaged with Christ in a work of "judgment" during the millennium, or the period of 1,000 years.

The Millennium Begins

How many resurrections are there to be?

"Do not marvel at this; for the hour is coming in which all who are in the graves will hear His voice and come forth—those who have done good, to *the resurrection of life,* and those who have done evil, to *the resurrection of condemnation.*" John 5:28, 29.

What class only have part in the first resurrection?

"*Blessed and holy* is he who has part in the first resurrection. Over such the second death has no power." Revelation 20:6.

What will Christ do with the saints when He comes?

"I will come again and *receive you to Myself; that where I am, there you may be also.*" John 14:3.

NOTE—In other words, Christ will take them to heaven, there to live and reign with Him during the 1,000 years.

Where did John, in vision, see the saints?

"After these things I looked, and behold, a great multitude which no one could number, of all nations, tribes, peoples,

and tongues, *standing before the throne and before the Lamb,* clothed with white robes, with palm branches in their hands." Revelation 7:9.

NOTE—This scripture shows plainly that the righteous are all taken to heaven immediately after the first resurrection. This accords with the words of Christ in John 14:1-3, where He says, "Let not your heart be troubled; you believe in God, believe also in Me. In My Father's house are many mansions; if it were not so, I would have told you. I go to prepare a place for you. And if I go and prepare a place for you, I will come again and *receive you to Myself; that where I am, there you may be also.*" Peter desired to accompany Christ to those mansions; but Jesus answered, "You cannot follow Me now, but *you shall follow Me afterward.*" John 13:36. This makes it clear that when Christ returns to earth to receive His people, He takes them to the Father's house in heaven.

What becomes of the living wicked when Christ comes?

"*As it was in the days of Noah,* so it will be also in the days of the Son of Man: They ate, they drank, they married wives, they were given in marriage, until the day that Noah entered the ark, and *the flood came and destroyed them all. Likewise as it was also in the days of Lot:* . . . on the day that Lot went out of Sodom it rained fire and brimstone from heaven and destroyed them all. *Even so will it be in the day when the Son of Man is revealed.*" Luke 17:26-30.

What does the apostle Paul say concerning this?

"When they say, 'Peace and safety!' *then sudden destruction comes upon them.* . . . And they shall not escape." 1 Thessalonians 5:3.

NOTE—When Christ comes, the righteous will be delivered and taken to heaven, and all the living wicked will be suddenly destroyed, as they were at the time of the Flood. For further proof, see 2 Thessalonians 1:7-9; Revelation 6:14-17; 19:11-21; Jeremiah 25:30-33. There will be no general resurrection of the wicked until the end of the 1,000 years. This will leave the earth desolate and without human inhabitants during this period.

How long is Satan to be imprisoned on this earth?

"I saw an angel coming down from heaven, having the key to the bottomless pit and a great chain in his hand. He laid hold of the dragon, that serpent of old, who is the Devil and Satan, and *bound him for a thousand years;* and he cast him into the bottomless pit, and shut him up, and set a seal on him, so that he should deceive the nations no more till the thousand years were finished." Revelation 20:1-3.

NOTE—The word rendered "bottomless pit" in this text is *abussos,* the Greek term employed by the Septuagint in Genesis 1:2, as the equivalent of the Hebrew word rendered "deep" in our English versions. A more literal translation would be "abyss." It is a term applied to the earth in its desolate, waste, chaotic, dark, uninhabited condition. In this condition it will remain during the 1,000 years. It will be the dreary prison house of Satan during this period. Here, in the midst of the moldering bones of wicked dead, slain at Christ's coming, the broken-down cities, and the wreck and ruin of all the pomp and power of this world, Satan will have opportunity to reflect upon the results of his rebellion against God.

Close of the Millennium

The righteous dead are raised at Christ's second coming. When will the rest of the dead, the wicked, be raised?

"The rest of the dead did not live again *until the thousand years were finished.*" Revelation 20:5.

NOTE—From this we see that the beginning and the close of the millennium, or 1,000 years, are marked by the two resurrections.

The word "millennium" is from two latin words, *mille,* meaning a "thousand," and *annus,* "year"—a thousand years. It covers the time during which Satan is to be bound and wicked human beings and angels are to be judged. This period is bounded by distinct events. Its beginning is marked by the close of probation, the pouring out of the seven last plagues, the second coming of Christ, and the resurrection of the righteous dead. It closes with the resurrection of the wicked, and their final destruction in the lake of fire. (See diagram on page 66.)

What change is made in Satan's condition at the close of the 1,000 years?

"After these things *he must be released for a little while.*" Verse 3.

NOTE—At the close of the 1,000 years Christ, accompanied by the saints, comes to the earth again, to execute judgment upon the wicked, and to prepare the earth, by a re-creation, for the eternal abode of the righteous. At this time, in answer to the summons of Christ, the wicked dead of all ages awake to life. This is the second resurrection, the resurrection unto damnation. The wicked come forth with the same rebellious spirit that possessed them in this life. Then Satan is loosed from his long period of captivity and inactivity.

As soon as the wicked are raised, what does Satan at once proceed to do?

"When the thousand years have expired, Satan will be released from his prison and will go out to *deceive the nations* which are in the four corners of the earth, Gog and Magog, *to gather them together to battle,* whose number is as the sand of the sea." Verses 7, 8.

Against whom do the wicked go to make war, and what is the outcome?

"They went up on the breadth of the earth and *surrounded the camp of the saints and the beloved city. And fire came down from God out of heaven and devoured them.*" Verse 9.

NOTE—This is the last act in the great controversy between Christ and Satan. The whole human race meet here for the first and last time. The eternal separation of the righteous from the wicked here takes place. At this time the judgment of God is executed upon the wicked in the lake of fire. This is the second death. This ends the great rebellion against God and His government. Now is heard the voice of God as He sits upon His throne, speaking to the saints, and saying, "Behold, I make all things new"; and out of the burning ruins of the old earth there springs forth before the admiring gaze of the millions of the redeemed "a new heaven and a new earth," in which they shall find an everlasting inheritance and dwelling place.

Conditions During the Millennium

What description does the prophet Jeremiah give of the earth during this time?

"I beheld the earth, and indeed it was *without form, and void;* and the heavens, they had no light. I beheld the mountains, and indeed they trembled, and all the hills moved back and forth. I beheld, and indeed *there was no man,* and all the birds of the heavens had fled. I beheld, and indeed *the fruitful land was a wilderness, and all its cities were broken down* at the presence of the Lord, by His fierce anger." Jeremiah 4:23-26.

NOTE—At the coming of Christ the earth is reduced to a chaotic state—to a mass of ruins. The heavens depart as a

Bible Answers

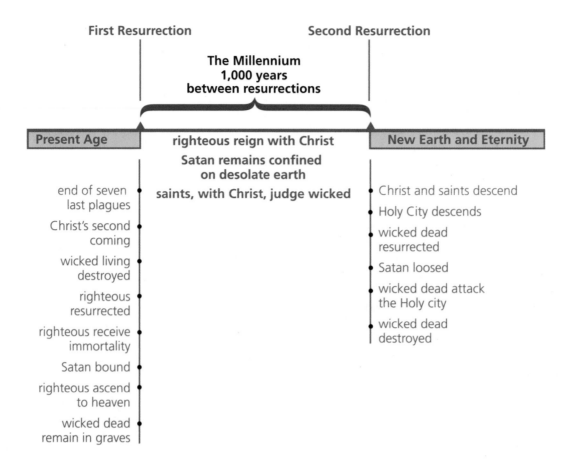

First Resurrection   **Second Resurrection**

**The Millennium
1,000 years
between resurrections**

| Present Age | righteous reign with Christ | New Earth and Eternity |

**Satan remains confined
on desolate earth**

saints, with Christ, judge wicked

Present Age column:
- end of seven last plagues
- Christ's second coming
- wicked living destroyed
- righteous resurrected
- righteous receive immortality
- Satan bound
- righteous ascend to heaven
- wicked dead remain in graves

New Earth and Eternity column:
- Christ and saints descend
- Holy City descends
- wicked dead resurrected
- Satan loosed
- wicked dead attack the Holy city
- wicked dead destroyed

---

scroll when it is rolled together; mountains are moved out of their places; and the earth is left a dark, dreary, desolate waste. (See Isaiah 24:1-3; Revelation 6:14-17.)

How does Isaiah speak of the wicked at this time?

"It shall come to pass in that day that the Lord will punish on high the host of exalted ones, and on the earth the kings of the earth. They will be gathered together, as prisoners are gathered in the pit, and *will be shut up in the prison;* after many days they will be punished." Isaiah 24:21, 22.

NOTE—The millennium is a great sabbath of rest, both for the earth and for God's people. For 6,000 years the earth and its inhabitants have been groaning under the curse of sin. The millennium, the seventh thousand, will be a sabbath of rest and release; for, says the prophet concerning the land, "as long as she lay desolate she kept *Sabbath.*" 2 Chronicles 36:21. "There remains therefore a rest for the people of God." Hebrews 4:9. This precedes the new-earth state.

The millennium is the closing period of God's great week of time—a great sabbath of rest to the earth and to the people of God.

It follows the close of the gospel age, and precedes the setting up of the everlasting kingdom of God on earth.

It comprehends what in the Scriptures is frequently spoken of as "the day of the Lord."

It is bounded at each end by a resurrection.

Its beginning is marked by the pouring out of the seven last plagues, the second coming of Christ, the resurrection of the righteous dead, the binding of Satan, and the translation of the saints to heaven; and its close, by the descent of the New Jerusalem, with Christ and the saints, from heaven, the resurrection of the wicked dead, the loosing of Satan, and the final destruction of the wicked.

During the 1,000 years the earth lies desolate; Satan and his angels are confined here; and the saints, with Christ, sit in judgment on the wicked, preparatory to their final punishment.

The wicked dead are then raised; Satan is loosed for a little season, and he and the host of the wicked encompass the camp of the saints and the Holy City, when fire comes down from God out of heaven and devours them. The earth is cleansed by the same fire that destroys the wicked, and, renewed, becomes the eternal abode of the saints.

The millennium is part of "the age to come." Its close will mark the beginning of the new-earth state.

Chapter 18

The Good News About
The Judgment

The 2300 Days of Daniel 8, 9

What startling message is given in Revelation 14:7?

"Fear God and give glory to Him, for the *hour of His judgment has come;* and worship Him who made heaven and earth, the sea and springs of water."

When is the hour of God's judgment according to the message given to Daniel?

"He said to me, 'For two thousand three hundred days; then the sanctuary shall be cleansed.'" Daniel 8:14.

NOTE—By the study of the succeeding chapters on the sanctuary, it will be seen that the cleansing of the sanctuary is the work of judgment. The Jewish people understood it so. This 2300-day period, being 2300 literal years (Ezekiel 4:6), reaches down to the cleansing of the sanctuary in heaven, or, in other words, to the time that the investigative judgment begins, as described in Daniel 7:9, 10.

Why was not this time period fully explained when the angel first appeared to Daniel?

"I, Daniel, fainted and was *sick for days;* afterward I arose and went about the king's business. I was astonished by the vision, but no one understood it." Daniel 8:27.

NOTE—The prophet had been given a vision of the great nations of his and succeeding days and the persecutions of God's people, concluding with the time period pointing to the cleansing of the sanctuary. But the aged Daniel fainted and was sick certain days. Consequently, the interpretation was arrested, and was not completed until after the recovery of the prophet. The vision and its partial explanation were given in the third year of Belshazzar's reign with his father, Nabonidus; the interpretation of the time period was given following the fall of Babylon, in the first year of Darius.

At some time subsequent to Daniel's recovery from his illness, to what did he turn his attention?

"In the first year of Darius . . . I, Daniel, understood by the books the number of the years specified by the word of the Lord through Jeremiah the prophet, that He would accomplish seventy years in the desolations of Jerusalem." Daniel 9:1, 2.

NOTE—Nebuchadnezzar besieged Jerusalem in the third year of Jehoiakim (Daniel 1:1), and Jeremiah announced the 70-year captivity in the fourth year of Jehoiakim (Jeremiah 25:1, 12). This means that the first deportation of the Jews of Babylon, when Daniel and his companions were carried away, was at that time. The seventy years of Jeremiah's prophecy would expire in 536 B.C. Since the first year of the Persian Empire began in 538 B.C., the restoration period was therefore only two years distant from the time.

What did this nearness of the time of restoration from captivity lead Daniel to do?

"I set my face toward the Lord God to make request by *prayer and supplications,* with fasting, sackcloth, and ashes." Daniel 9:3.

In what especially was the prophet interested?

"Now therefore, our God, hear the prayer of Your servant, and his supplications, and for the Lord's sake cause Your face to shine on Your *sanctuary, which is desolate.*" Verse 17.

Gabriel Again Appears

While Daniel was praying concerning the sanctuary lying desolate at Jerusalem, who appeared on the scene?

"Yes, while I was speaking in prayer, the man *Gabriel,* whom I had seen in the vision at the beginning, being caused to fly swiftly, reached me about the time of the evening offering." Verse 21.

NOTE—It was fitting that the angel Gabriel should return to the prophet for the purpose of explaining that portion of the prophecy in Daniel 8 that had not been interpreted, the time period, when Daniel was earnestly praying for the sanctuary made desolate at Jerusalem. The angel not only would open to his vision the earthly typical sanctuary and its future, but would give him, for the benefit of those living at the time of the end, a view of the true heavenly service.

Bible Answers

What did the angel at once ask the prophet to consider?

"He informed me, and talked with me, and said, 'O Daniel, I have now come forth to give you skill to understand. . . . Therefore consider the matter, and *understand the vision.*'" Daniel 9:22, 23.

NOTE—It is evident that the angel began just where he had left off in explanation of the prophecy of the eighth chapter; for he introduces no new line of prophecy, no new vision, "Consider *the* vision." In the Hebrew the definite article "the" here clearly specifies the vision previously mentioned. This is obviously the vision of the preceding chapter. Since the 2300-day period was the only part of the former vision left unexplained, the angel would naturally begin with an interpretation of that period.

What portion of the 2300 days mentioned in the vision was allotted to the Jews?

"*Seventy weeks* [literally, "*seventy sevens*"] are determined for your people and for your holy city." Verse 24.

NOTE—The word translated "weeks," literally, "sevens," is used in Jewish literature to refer to periods of seven days and also to periods of seven years. Jewish and Christian scholars, generally, have concluded that the context here requires that "weeks" of years be understood. "Seventy weeks" of seven years each would be 490 years.

In postbiblical Hebrew the word here translated "determined" had the meaning "to cut," "to cut off," "to determine," "to decree." In view of the fact that the 70 weeks of Daniel 9 are a part of the 2300 days of chapter 8, and were cut off from them and assigned particularly to the Jews, the meaning "to cut" here seems especially appropriate.

The 70 weeks, therefore, were "determined," or cut off. There are two periods of time under consideration: the first, the 2300-day period; the second, the 70-week period. They both had to do with the restoration of the Jewish people and the sanctuary, for the Jews were in captivity and the sanctuary was in ruins. The two periods must then begin with the restoration, and at the same time. The full restoration of the Jewish laws and government pertaining to the people and their sanctuary took place in 457 B.C., as we shall see later. It is reasonable, then, to say that the 70 weeks were a part of the 2300-year period, and that they were thus "cut off" as a period pertaining to the Jewish people and their sanctuary service.

What was to be accomplished at or near the close of this 70-week period?

"Seventy weeks are determined for your people and for your holy city, to finish the transgression, to make an end of sins, to make reconciliation for iniquity, to bring in everlasting righteousness, to seal up vision and prophecy, and to anoint the Most Holy." Verse 24.

NOTE—"*To Finish the Transgression.*"—The Jews were to fill up the measure of their iniquity by rejecting and crucifying the Messiah; they would then no longer be His peculiar, chosen people. Read Matthew 21:38-48; 23:32-38; 27:25.

"*To Make an End of Sins.*"—The best explanation of this clause is given in Hebrews 9:26: "But now, once at the end of the ages, He has appeared to put away sin by the sacrifice of Himself"; and in Romans 8:3: "For what the law could not do in that it was weak through the flesh, God did by sending His own Son in the likeness of sinful flesh, on account of sin: He condemned sin in the flesh."

"*To Bring in Everlasting Righteousness.*"—This must mean the righteousness of Christ—that righteousness by which He was enabled to make an atonement for sin, and which, through faith, may be imputed to the penitent believer.

"*To Anoint the Most Holy.*"—The Hebrew words here used are regularly employed of the sanctuary, but not of persons. The anointing of the "Most Holy," then, must refer to the anointing of the heavenly sanctuary, when Christ became the "Minister of the sanctuary and of the true tabernacle which the Lord erected, and not man." Hebrews 8:2.

The Beginning of the Time Period

When did the angel say that the 70 weeks were to begin?

"Know therefore and understand, that from the going forth of the command to restore and build Jerusalem until Messiah the Prince, there shall be seven weeks and sixty-two weeks; the street shall be built again, and the wall, even in troublesome times." Daniel 9:25.

NOTE—Seventy weeks would be a period of 490 literal years. Sixty-nine (seven weeks and 62 weeks) of the 70 weeks were to reach "until the Messiah the Prince." *Messiah* is Christ, "the Anointed." *Messiah* is the Hebrew word, and *Christ* the Greek word, meaning "anointed."

How was Jesus anointed?

"God anointed Jesus of Nazareth with the Holy Spirit and with power." Acts 10:38.

At what time did Jesus receive the special anointing of the Holy Spirit?

"Jesus also was baptized; and while He prayed, the heaven was opened. And the Holy Spirit descended in bodily form like a dove upon Him, and a voice came from heaven which

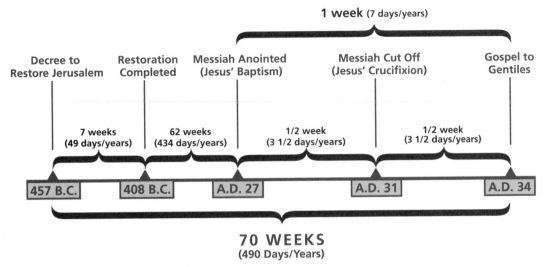

said, 'You are My beloved Son; in You I am well pleased.'" Luke 3:21, 22.

What prophecy did Jesus quote shortly after this as applying to Himself?

"The Spirit of the Lord is upon Me, because He has anointed Me to preach the gospel to the poor." Luke 4:18. (See Mark 1:15.)

NOTE—It is evident that the 69 weeks (483 years) were to reach to the baptism of Christ, as that was the time of His anointing by the Holy Spirit. John the Baptist began his work in the fifteenth year of the reign of Tiberius (Luke 3:1-3), and this would put the anointing of Jesus in A.D. 27, at the time of His baptism.

When was the decree made to restore and build Jerusalem?

"This Ezra came up from Babylon. . . . Some of the children of Israel, the priests, the Levites, the singers, the gatekeepers, and the Nethinim came up to Jerusalem in the seventh year of King Artaxerxes. And Ezra came to Jerusalem in the fifth month, which was in the seventh year of the king." Ezra 7:6-8.

NOTE—Three decrees were issued by Persian monarchs for the restoration of the Jews to their homeland. They are mentioned in the book of Ezra: "They built and finished it, according to the commandment of the God of Israel, and according to the command of Cyrus, Darius, and Artaxerxes king of Persia." Ezra 6:14.

The decree of Cyrus pertained to the Temple only; the decree of Darius Hystaspes provided for the continuance of that work, hindered by Smerdis: but the decree of Artaxerxes restored the full Jewish government, making provision for the enforcement of their laws. This last decree, therefore, is the one from which we reckon the 70 weeks, as well as the 2300 days.

The letter of Artaxerxes to Ezra, conferring upon him authority to do his work, is found in Ezra 7:11-26.

The decree of Artaxerxes was issued in the seventh year of his reign, and according to ancient methods of chronology, went into effect in Jerusalem in the fall of 457 B.C. Reckoning 483 full years from the first day of 457 B.C. would bring us to the last day of A.D. 26. This is demonstrated from the fact that it requires all of the 26 years A.D. and all of the 457 years B.C. to make 483 years, which may be illustrated by the diagram above.

The diagram also reveals that if the decree for the complete restoration of Jerusalem did not go into effect until after Ezra reached Jerusalem, that is, until past the middle of the year 457 B.C. (Ezra 7:8), then all the time of the first part of that year not included in the period must be added to the last day of A.D. 26, which would bring us to the latter part of A.D. 27, the time of Christ's baptism. This "seals up," or makes sure, the prophecy.

At the close of 483 years, in A.D. 27, one week, or seven years of the 490, yet remained. What was to be done in the midst of that week?

"He shall confirm a covenant with many for one week; but in the middle of the week He shall bring an end to sacrifice and offering." Daniel 9:27.

NOTE—As the 69 weeks ended in the fall of A.D. 27, the middle of the seventieth week, or the three and a half years, would end in the spring of A.D. 31, when Christ was crucified, and by His death caused to cease, or brought to an end, the sacrifices and oblations of the earthy sanctuary. Three and a half years more (the last part of the seventieth week) would end in the autumn of A.D. 34. This brings us to the end of the 490 years that were "cut off" from the 2300. There still remain 1810 years, which, if added to A.D. 34, take us to A.D. 1844.

Bible Answers

A.D. 1844 and the Investigative Judgment

And what did the angel say would then take place?

"He said to me, 'For two thousand three hundred days; then the sanctuary shall be cleansed.'" Daniel 8:14.

NOTE—This diagram below delineates the longest time prophecy in the Bible. Since in Bible prophecy a day represents a literal year (Numbers 14:34; Ezekiel 4:6), the 2300-day prophecy of Daniel 8:14 points out 23 centuries of history from Artaxerxes' commandment to restore and rebuild Jerusalem down to A.D. 1844, when the atonement, or investigative judgment, the great closing work of Christ for the world, began in the heavenly sanctuary. The typical Day of Atonement for Israel occupied but one day in a year. This may occupy but a correspondingly short time. Already that work has been going on for more than a century, and must soon close. Who is ready to meet its decisions?

Under what symbol is the importance of the judgment-hour message emphasized?

"I saw another *angel flying in the midst of heaven,* having the everlasting gospel to preach to those who dwell on the earth—to every nation, tribe, tongue, and people—*saying with a loud voice,* 'Fear God and give glory to Him, for the hour of His judgment has come.'" Revelation 14:6, 7.

NOTE—The symbol of an angel is here used to represent the message of the judgment that is to be preached to every nation. Since angels preach their messages to human beings through human agencies, it would be understood that this symbol of an angel flying in midheaven represents a great religious movement giving to humanity the judgment-hour message.

In view of the investigative judgment, what are we admonished to do?

"*Fear God and give glory to Him,* for the hour of His judgment has come; and *worship Him who made heaven and earth, the sea and springs of water.*" Verse 7.

What earnest admonition is given by the apostle Paul?

"These times of ignorance God overlooked, but now *commands all men everywhere to repent,* because He has appointed a day on which He will judge the world in righteousness by the Man whom He has ordained. He has given assurance of this to all by raising Him from the dead." Acts 17:30, 31.

The Sanctuary and Two Apartments

What did God command Israel to make?

"And let them make Me a *sanctuary,* that I may dwell among them." Exodus 25:8.

What was offered in this sanctuary?

"In which both gifts and sacrifices are offered." Hebrews 9:9.

Besides the court, how many parts had this sanctuary?

"The veil shall be a divider for you between the *holy place* and the *Most Holy.*" Exodus 26:33.

What was in the first apartment, or holy place?

"For a tabernacle was prepared: the first part, in which was the *lampstand,* the *table,* and the *showbread,* which is called the sanctuary." Hebrews 9:2. "He put the gold altar in the tabernacle of meeting in front of the veil." Exodus 40:26. (See also Exodus 30:1-6.)

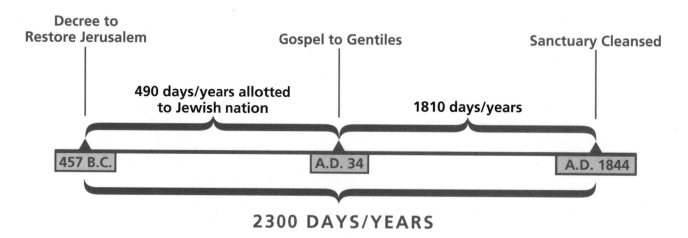

Decree to **Restore Jerusalem** — **Gospel to Gentiles** — **Sanctuary Cleansed**

490 days/years allotted to Jewish nation

1810 days/years

457 B.C.   A.D. 34   A.D. 1844

2300 DAYS/YEARS

What was contained in the second apartment?

"And behind the second veil, the part of the tabernacle which is called the Holiest of All, which had the *golden censer and the ark of the covenant* overlaid on all sides with gold, in which were . . . the tablets of the covenant." Hebrews 9:3, 4. (See also Exodus 40:20, 21.)

By what name was the cover of the ark known?

"You shall put *the mercy seat* on top of the ark, and in the ark you shall put the Testimony that I will give you." Exodus 25:21.

Where was God to meet with Israel?

"And there I will meet with you, and I will speak with you *from above the mercy seat, from between the two cherubim which are on the ark of the Testimony.*" Verse 22.

What was in the ark, under the mercy seat?

"And He wrote on the tablets according to the first writing, *the Ten Commandments. . . .* Then I turned and came down from the mountain, and *put the tablets in the ark* which I had made." Deuteronomy 10:4, 5.

When did the priest minister in the first apartment?

"Now when these things had been thus prepared, the priests *always* went into the first part of the tabernacle, performing the services." Hebrews 9:6.

Who went into the second apartment? When and why?

"But into the second part *the high priest went alone once a year, not without blood, which he offered for himself and for the people's sins committed* in ignorance." Verse 7.

The Daily Service

What were sinners desiring pardon instructed to do?

"If anyone of the common people sins unintentionally by doing something against any of the commandments of the Lord . . . , then he shall bring as his offering a kid of the goats, a female without blemish, for his sin which he has committed. *And he shall lay his hand on the head of the sin offering, and kill the sin offering at the place of the burnt offering.*" Leviticus 4:27-29.

NOTE—According to this, those who sinned in Israel violated one of the Ten Commandments that were in the ark under the mercy seat. These commandments are the foundation of God's government. To violate them is to commit sin, and so become subject to death. (1 John 3:4; Romans 6:23.) But there was a mercy seat reared above these holy and just commandments. In the dispensation of His mercy God grants the sinner the privilege of confessing sins and bringing a substitute to meet the demands of the law, and thus of obtaining mercy.

What was done with the blood of the offering?

"The priest shall take some of its blood with his finger, put it on the horns of the altar of burnt offering, and *pour all the remaining blood at the base of the altar.*" Leviticus 4:30.

NOTE—Persons who discovered their sin by the law that demanded the death of the transgressor first brought an offering; then they confessed their sin while laying their hands on the head of the victim, thus, in figure, transferring their sin to the victim; the victim was next slain in the court, or outer part of the sanctuary, and its blood put on the horns of the altar and poured at the foot of the altar. In this way sins were pardoned, and, in the typical service, transferred to the sanctuary.

The Day of Atonement

After this accumulation of the sins of the year, what service took place yearly on the tenth day of the seventh month?

"This shall be a statute forever for you: In the seventh month, on the tenth day of the month, you shall afflict your souls. . . . For *on that day the priest shall make atonement for you, to cleanse you, that you may be clean from all your sins before the Lord.*" Leviticus 16:29, 30.

How was the sanctuary itself to be cleansed, and how were the sins of the people to be finally disposed of?

"And he [the high priest] shall take from the congregation of the children of Israel two kids of the goats as a sin offering. . . . He shall take the two goats and present them before the Lord at the door of the tabernacle of meeting. Then Aaron shall cast lots for the two goats: one lot *for the Lord* and the other lot *for the scapegoat.*" Verses 5-8.

NOTE—The Hebrew word for scapegoat is *Azazel.* It is used as a proper name, and, according to the opinion of the most ancient Hebrews and Christians, refers to Satan, or the angel who revolted and persisted in rebellion and sin.

What was done with the blood of the goat upon which the Lord's lot fell?

"Then he shall kill the goat of the sin offering, which is for the people, bring its blood inside the veil, *and sprinkle it on the mercy seat* and before the mercy seat." Verse 15.

Why was it necessary to make this atonement?

"So he shall make atonement for the Holy Place, because of the uncleanness of the children of Israel, and because of their transgressions, for all their sins; and so he shall do for the tabernacle of meeting which remains among them in the midst of their uncleanness." Verse 16.

NOTE—Sins were transferred to the sanctuary during the year by the blood and flesh of the sin offerings made daily at the door of the tabernacle. Here they remained until the Day of Atonement, when the high priest went into the Most Holy Place with the blood of the goat on which the Lord's lot fell; and, bearing the accumulated sins of the year in before the mercy seat, he there, in type, atoned for them, and so cleansed the sanctuary.

After having made atonement for the people in the Most Holy Place, what did the high priest next do?

"And when he has made an end of atoning for the Holy Place, the tabernacle of meeting, and the altar, he shall bring the live goat. Aaron shall lay both his hands on the head of the live goat, confess over it all the iniquities of the children of Israel, and all their transgressions, concerning all their sins, putting them on the head of the goat, and shall send it away into the wilderness by the hand of a suitable man. The goat shall bear on itself all their iniquities to an uninhabited land; and he shall release the goat in the wilderness." Verses 20-22.

NOTE—The offering of the Lord's goat cleansed the sanctuary. By this offering the sins of the people, transferred there during the year, were, in type, atoned for; but they were not by this offering finally disposed of, or destroyed. The scapegoat, symbolizing Satan, the great tempter and originator of sin, was brought to the sanctuary, and upon his head were placed these already atoned-for sins. The sending away of the goat into the wilderness separated the sins forever from the people. (On the scapegoat, see John McClintock and James Strong, *Cyclopaedia of Biblical, Theological, and Ecclesiastical Literature,* vol. 9, pp. 397, 398, art. "Scapegoat"; *The Encyclopedic Dictionary,* vol. 1, p. 397; *The New Schaff-Herzog Encyclopedia of Religious Knowledge,* vol. 1, p. 389, art. "Azazel.")

A Type of the Heavenly Sanctuary

What was this earthly sanctuary and its round of service?

"It was *symbolic* for the present time." Hebrews 9:9.

Of what sanctuary, or tabernacle, is Christ the minister?

"A Minister of the sanctuary and of the true tabernacle *which the Lord erected, and not man.*" Hebrews 8:2.

Of what was the blood of all the sacrifices of the former dispensation only a type?

"Not with the blood of goats and calves, but *with His own blood* He entered the Most Holy Place once for all, having obtained eternal redemption." Hebrews 9:12. (See Ephesians 5:2.)

NOTE—Through the sacrifices and offerings brought to the altar of the earthly sanctuary, the penitent believer was to lay hold of the merits of Christ, the Savior to come. In this way, and in this way only, was there any virtue connected with them.

At Christ's death, what miracle signified that the priestly services of the earthly sanctuary were finished?

"And Jesus cried out again with a loud voice, and yielded up His spirit. Then, behold, *the veil of the temple was torn in two from top to bottom.*" Matthew 27:50, 51.

NOTE—Type had met antitype; the shadow had reached the substance. Christ, the great sacrifice, had been slain, and was now to enter upon His work as our great high priest in the sanctuary in heaven. The priestly work in the earthly sanctuary was typical of the work of Christ in the heavenly sanctuary.

How are the heavenly and earthly sanctuaries related?

"Who serve the *copy* and *shadow* of the heavenly things, as Moses was divinely instructed when he was about to make the tabernacle. For He said, 'See that you make all things according to the *pattern* shown you on the mountain.'" Hebrews 8:5.

By what comparison is it shown that the heavenly sanctuary will be cleansed?

"Therefore it was necessary that the copies of the things in the heavens should be purified with these, *but the heavenly things themselves with better sacrifices than these.*" Hebrews 9:23.

When Christ has finished His priestly mediatorial work in the heavenly sanctuary, what decree will go forth?

"He who is unjust, let him be unjust still; he who is filthy, let him be filthy still; he who is righteous, let him be righteous still; he who is holy, let him be holy still." Revelation 22:11.

NOTE—This declaration is made immediately before the coming of Christ in the clouds of heaven.

According to Daniel's vision of the judgment, what is to be given to Christ while He is still before the Father?

"I was watching in the night visions, and behold, One like the Son of Man, coming with the clouds of heaven! He came to the Ancient of Days, and they brought Him near before Him.

Then to Him was given *dominion* and *glory* and *a kingdom*, that all peoples, nations, and languages should serve Him." Daniel 7:13, 14.

What will occur when the Lord descends from heaven?

"For the Lord Himself will descend from heaven with a shout, with the voice of an archangel, and with the trumpet of God. And *the dead in Christ will rise first. Then we who are alive and remain shall be caught up together with them in the clouds to meet the Lord in the air.* And thus we shall always be with the Lord." 1 Thessalonians 4:16, 17.

What statement immediately following the announcement mentioned in Revelation 22:11 indicates that a judgment work has been in progress before Christ comes?

"And behold, I am coming quickly, and *My reward is with Me, to give to every one according to his work.*" Verse 12.

NOTE—The typical sanctuary service is fully met in the work of Christ. As the atonement day of the former dispensation was really a day of judgment, so the atonement work of Christ will include the investigation of the cases of His people prior to His coming the second time to receive them unto Himself.

Nature and Time of the Message

What prophetic view of the judgment was given Daniel?

"I watched till thrones were put in place, and the Ancient of Days was seated. . . . A thousand thousands ministered to Him; ten thousand times ten thousand stood before Him. The court was seated, and the books were opened." Daniel 7:9, 10.

What assurance of the judgment has God given?

"Because *He has appointed a day on which He will judge the world* in righteousness by the Man whom He has ordained. He has given assurance of this to all *by raising Him from the dead.*" Acts 17:31.

What message announces that the judgment hour has come?

"Then I saw another angel flying in the midst of heaven, having the everlasting gospel to preach to those who dwell on the earth—to every nation, tribe, tongue, and people—saying with a loud voice, 'Fear God and give glory to Him, for *the hour of His judgment has come;* and worship Him who made heaven and earth, the sea and springs of water.'" Revelation 14:6, 7.

In view of the judgment hour, what is proclaimed anew?

"The everlasting gospel." Verse 6.

How extensively is this message to be proclaimed?

"To *every nation, tribe, tongue,* and *people.*" Verse 6.

What is the whole world called upon to do?

"Fear God and give glory to Him." Verse 7.

What special reason is given for this?

"For *the hour of His judgment has come.*" Verse 7.

Whom are all called upon to worship?

"Him who made heaven and earth." Verse 7.

Bible Answers

NOTE—There is only one gospel (Romans 1:16, 17; Galatians 1:8), first announced in Eden (Genesis 3:15), preached to Abraham (Galatians 3:8) and to the children of Israel (Hebrews 4:1, 2), and proclaimed anew in every generation. In its development the gospel meets the needs of every crisis in the world's history. John the Baptist in his preaching announced the kingdom to heaven at hand (Matthew 3:1, 2), and prepared the way for the First Advent. (John 1:22, 23.) Christ Himself, in His preaching of the gospel, announced the fulfillment of a definite-time prophecy (the 69 weeks, or 483 years, of Daniel 9:25), and called the people to repentance, in view of the coming of the predicted Messiah. (Mark 1:14, 15.) So when the time for the judgment comes, and Christ's second advent is near, a worldwide announcement of these events is to be made in the preaching of the everlasting gospel adapted to meet the need of the hour.

What prophetic period extends to the time of the cleansing of the sanctuary, or the investigative judgment?

"And he said to me, 'For *two thousand three hundred days;* then the sanctuary shall be cleansed.'" Daniel 8:14.

When did this long period expire?

In A.D. 1844. See page 70.

NOTE—The whole period extends to the time of the judgment, just preceding the Second Advent, and at its expiration a special gospel message is sent to all the world, proclaiming the judgment hour at hand and calling upon all to worship the Creator. The facts of history answer to this interpretation of the prophecy, for at this very time (1844) just such a message was being proclaimed in various parts of the world. This was the beginning of the great Second Advent message that is now being proclaimed throughout the world.

Call to Worship the Creator

How is the true God distinguished from all false gods?

"Thus you shall say to them: 'The *gods that have not made the heavens and the earth* shall perish from the earth. . . .' *He [the true God] has made the earth by His power, He has established the world by His wisdom, and has stretched out the heavens at His discretion.*" Jeremiah 10:11, 12.

For what reason is worship justly due God?

"For the Lord is the great God, and the great King above all gods. . . . *The sea is His, for He made it; and His hands formed the dry land.* Oh come, let us worship and bow down; let us kneel before the Lord our Maker. Psalm 95:3-6.

Why do the inhabitants of heaven worship God?

"The twenty-four elders fall down before Him . . . , saying: 'You are worthy, O Lord, to receive glory and honor and power; *for You created all things,* and by Your will they exist and were created.'" Revelation 4:10, 11.

What memorial of His creative power did God establish?

"Remember *the Sabbath day,* to keep it holy. . . . *For in six days the Lord made the heavens and the earth, the sea, and all that is in them,* and rested the seventh day. Therefore the Lord blessed the Sabbath day and hallowed it." Exodus 20:8-11.

What place has the Sabbath in the work of salvation?

"Moreover I also gave them My Sabbaths, to be *a sign* between them and Me, that they might know that I am the Lord who *sanctifies* them." Ezekiel 20:12.

The Standard for All

How many are concerned in the judgment?

"For we must *all* appear before the judgment seat of Christ, that *each one* may receive the things done in the body, *according to what he has done, whether good or bad.*" 2 Corinthians 5:10.

What will be the standard in the judgment?

"For whoever shall keep the whole law, and yet stumble in one point, he is guilty of all. For He who said, 'Do not commit adultery,' also said, 'Do not murder.' Now if you do not commit adultery, but you do murder, you have become a transgressor of the law. So speak and so do as those who will be judged *by the law of liberty.*" James 2:10-12.

In view of the judgment, what exhortation is given?

"Let us hear the conclusion of the whole matter: *Fear God and keep His commandments,* for this is man's all. For God will bring every work into judgment, including every secret thing, whether good or evil." Ecclesiastes 12:13, 14.

NOTE—A comparison of Revelation 14:7 with Ecclesiastes 12:13 suggests that the way to give glory to God is to keep His commandments, and that in giving the judgment-hour message, the duty of keeping the commandments would be emphasized. This is plainly shown in the description given of the people who are gathered out of every nation, kindred, tongue, and people as the result of the preaching of this message, in connection with other messages which immediately follow and accompany it. Of this people it is said: "Here are those who keep the commandments of God and the faith of Jesus." Revelation 14:12.

Chapter 19

The Good News About
Growth in Christ

Grace Multiplied

How does the apostle Peter close his second epistle?

"But *grow in the grace* and knowledge of our Lord and Savior Jesus Christ." 2 Peter 3:18.

How may grace and peace be multiplied in believers?

"Grace and peace be multiplied to you *in the knowledge of God and of Jesus our Lord.*" 2 Peter 1:2.

What is implied in a knowledge of God and Jesus Christ?

"And *this is eternal life,* that they may know You, the only true God, and Jesus Christ whom You have sent." John 17:3.

By what may we be partakers of the divine nature?

"By which have been given to us *exceedingly great and precious promises,* that through these you may be partakers of the divine nature, having escaped the corruption that is in the world through lust." 2 Peter 1:4.

Grace by Addition

What graces are we to add in our character building?

"But also for this very reason, giving all diligence, add to your faith *virtue,* to virtue *knowledge,* to knowledge *self-control,* to self-control *perseverance,* to perseverance *godliness,* to godliness *brotherly kindness,* and to brotherly kindness *love.*" Verses 5-7.

NOTE—*Faith* is the first round in the Christian ladder, the first step Godward. "He who comes to God must *believe.*" Hebrews 11:6.

But an inoperative faith is useless. "Faith without *works* is dead." James 2:20. To be of value, there must be coupled with faith *virtue,* or *moral excellence.*

To moral excellence there needs to be added *knowledge;* otherwise, like the stumbling Jews, one may have a zeal, "but *not according to knowledge.*" Romans 10:2. Fanaticism is the result of such courage, or zeal. Knowledge, therefore, is an essential to healthy Christian growth.

To knowledge there needs to be added *temperance,*

or *self-control—self-government.* To know to do good, and not do it, is as useless as is faith without works. (See James 4:17.)

Patience, or *steadfast endurance,* naturally follows *temperance,* or *self-control.* It is well-nigh impossible for an intemperate person to be *patient.*

Having gained control of oneself, and become patient, one is in a condition to manifest *godliness,* or *Godlikeness.*

Kindness toward the brethren, or *brotherly kindness,* naturally follows godliness.

Charity, or love for *all,* even our *enemies,* is the crowning grace, the highest step, the eighth round, in the Christian ladder.

The arrangement in this enumeration of graces is by no means accidental or haphazard, but logical and sequential, each following the other in natural, necessary order. The finger of Inspiration is seen here.

What is said of charity in the Scriptures?

"Love *suffers long and is kind; . . . thinks no evil; does not rejoice in iniquity, but rejoices in the truth; bears all things, believes all things, hopes all things, endures all things.*" 1 Corinthians 13:4-7. "And above all things have fervent love for one another, for *'love will cover a multitude of sins.'*" 1 Peter 4:8.

NOTE—"Charity" and "love" are translations of the same Greek word. Instead of "charity" most versions read "love."

What is charity called?

"But above all these things put on love, which is *the bond of perfection.*" Colossians 3:14.

What is the result of cultivating these eight graces?

"For if these things are yours and abound, you will be neither barren nor unfruitful in the knowledge of our Lord Jesus Christ." 2 Peter 1:8.

What is the condition of one who lacks these graces?

"For he who lacks these things *is shortsighted, even to blindness, and has forgotten that he was cleansed from his old sins.*" Verse 9.

Bible Answers

What is promised those who add grace to grace?

"If you do these things *you will never stumble.*" Verse 10.

What power was to make war upon the remnant church prior to the second advent of the Savior to this earth?

"And *the dragon* [Satan] was enraged with the woman, and he went to make war with the rest of her offspring, who keep the commandments of God and have the testimony of Jesus Christ." Revelation 12:17.

What reward is promised to all who overcome each besetting sin?

"To him who overcomes I will *give to eat from the tree of life,* which is in the midst of the Paradise of God." Revelation 2:7. (See also Revelation 2:11, 17, 26-28; 3:5, 12, 21.) "He who overcomes shall inherit *all things.*" Revelation 21:7.

The Conquering Leader

Through whom are we able to conquer the power that wars against us?

"Yet in all these things we are more than conquerors *through Him who loved us.*" Romans 8:37.

Who was the invisible leader of the armies of Israel?

"And it came to pass, when Joshua was by Jericho, that he lifted his eyes and looked, and behold, a Man stood opposite him with His sword drawn in His hand. And Joshua went to Him and said to Him, 'Are You for us or for our adversaries?' So He said, 'No, but as *Commander of the army of the Lord* I have now come.'" Joshua 5:13, 14. (See also 1 Corinthians 10:1-4.)

Weapons for Warfare

What is the character of the Christian's weapons of warfare?

"For the weapons of our warfare are *not carnal but mighty in God for pulling down strongholds.*" 2 Corinthians 10:4.

What are these weapons able to conquer?

"Casting down *arguments* and *every high thing that exalts itself against the knowledge of God,* bringing every thought into captivity to the obedience of Christ." Verse 5.

What are we to put on?

"*Put on the whole armor of God,* that you may be able to stand against the wiles of the devil." Ephesians 6:11.

With what kind of forces do we have to contend?

"For we do not wrestle against flesh and blood, but against *principalities,* against *powers,* against *the rulers of the darkness of this age,* against *spiritual hosts of wickedness in the heavenly places.*" Verse 12.

NOTE—"Spiritual hosts of wickedness in the heavenly places" is more accurately rendered "wicked spirits in heavenly places."

What are the first essentials of the needed armor?

"Stand therefore, having *girded your waist with truth,* having put on the *breastplate of righteousness.*" Verse 14.

With what are the feet of the children of God to be shod?

"And having shod your feet with *the preparation of the gospel of peace.*" Verse 15. (See also Ephesians 2:14; James 3:18.)

What piece of armor is next mentioned as necessary?

"Above all, taking *the shield of faith* with which you will be able to quench all the fiery darts of the wicked one." Ephesians 6:16. (See 1 John 5:4; Hebrews 11:6.)

What armor is to be put on as a protection to the head?

"And take *the helmet of salvation.*" Ephesians 6:17.

NOTE—In 1 Thessalonians 5:8 the helmet is called "the *hope* of salvation." The helmet was worn to protect the head. So the hope of salvation will preserve the courage, and thus aid in protecting the spiritual life of the Christian pilgrim when beset by the enemy of righteousness.

What is the sword of the Christian soldier?

"*The sword of the Spirit,* which is *the word of God.*" Ephesians 6:17.

NOTE—By this Christ defeated the enemy. (See Matthew 4:1-11; Luke 4:1-13.) But no one can *use this sword* who does not *know* it. Hence, the importance of studying and knowing for oneself what the Bible teaches.

Faithfulness and Victory

In what words are the courage, faithfulness, and loyalty of the church expressed?

"And they overcame him by the blood of the Lamb and by the word of their testimony, and *they did not love their lives to the death.*" Revelation 12:11.

Will Christ's loyal soldiers be victorious under Him?

"And I saw something like a sea of glass mingled with fire, and those who *have the victory* over the beast, over his image and over his mark and over the number of his name, standing on the sea of glass, having harps of God." Revelation 15:2.

God's Promises Regarding Prayer

By what title does the psalmist address God?

"*O You who hear prayer,* to You all flesh will come." Psalm 65:2.

Of whom does the Bible teach that God is a rewarder?

"A rewarder *of those who diligently seek Him.*" Hebrews 11:6.

How willing is God to hear and answer prayer?

"If you then, being evil, know how to give good gifts to your children, *how much more will your Father who is in heaven give good things to those who ask Him!*" Matthew 7:11.

What above all else shows God's willingness to do this?

"He who did not spare His own Son, but delivered Him up for us all, how shall He not with Him also freely give us all things?" Romans 8:32.

The First Step In Prayer

Upon what conditions are we promised needed blessings?

"*Ask,* and it will be given to you; *seek,* and you will find; *knock,* and it will be opened to you. For everyone who asks receives, and he who seeks finds, and to him who knocks it will be opened." Matthew 7:7, 8.

NOTE—"Prayer is the opening of the heart to God as to a friend."—E. G. White, *Steps to Christ* (pocket ed.), p. 93. Prayer does not change God; but it does change *us* and *our relation* to God. It places us in the channel of blessings, and in that frame of mind in which God can consistently and safely grant our requests.

"How shall we pray so as to be heard and to receive help? For one thing, there must be a real desire in our hearts. Forms of words do not make prayer: we must want something and must realize our dependence upon God for it."—J. R. Miller.

From whom do all good and perfect gifts come?

"Every good gift and every perfect gift is from above, and comes down from *the Father of lights,* with whom there is no variation or shadow of turning." James 1:17.

If one lacks wisdom, what is that person told to do?

"If any of you lacks wisdom, *let him ask of God,* who gives to all liberally and without reproach, and it will be given to him." Verse 5.

Three Conditions to Answered Prayer

How must one ask in order to receive?

"But let him *ask in faith, with no doubting,* for he who doubts is like a wave of the sea driven and tossed by the wind. For let not that man suppose that he will receive anything from the Lord." Verses 6, 7. (See Mark 11:24.)

Under what condition does the Lord not hear prayer?

"*If I regard iniquity in my heart,* the Lord will not hear." Psalm 66:18. (See Isaiah 59:1, 2; James 4:3.)

Whose prayers does Solomon say are an abomination?

"*One who turns away his ear from hearing the law, even his prayer is an abomination.*" Proverbs 28:9.

NOTE—Contention and discord quench the spirit of prayer. (1 Peter 3:1-7.) Many grieve the Spirit and drive Christ from their homes by giving way to impatience and passion. Angels of God flee from homes where there are unkind words, contention, and strife.

For whom did Christ teach us to pray?

"But I say to you, love your enemies, bless those who curse you, do good to those who hate you, and *pray for those who spitefully use you and persecute you.*" Matthew 5:44.

NOTE—We cannot hate those for whom we pray sincerely.

When we are praying, what must we do in order to be forgiven?

"And whenever you stand praying, *if you have anything against anyone, forgive him,* that your Father in heaven may also forgive you your trespasses." Mark 11:25.

Time, Place, and Content of Prayer

What did Christ say concerning secret prayer?

"But you, when you pray, *go into your room,* and when you have shut your door, *pray to your Father who is in the* secret place; and your Father who sees in secret will reward you openly." Matthew 6:6.

To what place did Jesus retire for secret devotion?

"And when He had sent the multitudes away, *He went up on the mountain by Himself to pray.* Now when evening came, He was alone there." Matthew 14:23.

With what should our prayers be mingled?

"Be anxious for nothing, but in everything by prayer and supplication, *with thanksgiving,* let your requests be made known to God." Philippians 4:6.

How often should we pray?

"*Praying always* with all prayer and supplication in the Spirit." Ephesians 6:18. "*Pray without ceasing.*" 1 Thessalonians 5:17. "*Every day I will bless You,* and I will praise Your name forever and ever." Psalm 145:2.

The psalmist said he would pray how often?

"*Evening* and *morning* and at *noon* I will pray, and cry aloud, and He shall hear my voice." Psalm 55:17. (See Daniel 6:10.)

In whose name did Christ teach us to pray?

"And whatever you ask in *My name,* that I will do." John 14:13.

Why did the unjust judge answer the widow's prayer?

"Though I do not fear God nor regard man, yet *because this widow troubles me* I will avenge her, lest *by her continual coming she weary me.*" Luke 18:4, 5.

NOTE—The lesson of the parable is that "men always ought to pray and not lose heart." Verse 1. If this woman, by her persistence in asking, obtained her request from such a man, surely God, who is just, will answer the earnest, persistent prayers of His people, though the answer may be long delayed.

Subjects of Meditation

What was one of Paul's injunctions to Timothy?

"*Meditate on these things;* give yourself entirely to them." 1 Timothy 4:15.

NOTE—Meditation is to the soul what digestion is to the body. It assimilates, appropriates, and makes personal and practical that which has been seen, heard, or read.

When would the psalmist praise God with joyful lips?

"*When I remember You* on my bed, *I meditate on You* in the night watches." Psalm 63:6.

How will such meditation be to one who loved God?

"May my meditation be *sweet* to Him." Psalm 104:34.

In what, says the psalmist, does the man who is blessed delight and meditate?

"But his delight is in *the law of the Lord,* and in *His law* he meditates day and night." Psalm 1:2.

Temptation and Meditation

With what adversary do we constantly have to contend?

"Be sober, be vigilant; because *your adversary the devil* walks about like a roaring lion, seeking whom he may devour." 1 Peter 5:8.

When is a person tempted?

"But each one is tempted when *he is drawn away by his own desires and enticed.*" James 1:14.

That we may not be overcome, what are we told to do?

"*Watch and pray, lest you enter into temptation.* The spirit indeed is willing, but the flesh is weak." Matthew 26:41.

Necessity of Constant Prayer Attitude

How constantly should we pray?

"Pray *without ceasing.*" 1 Thessalonians 5:17. "Continuing *steadfastly in prayer.*" Romans 12:12.

NOTE—This does not mean that we should be constantly bowed before God in prayer, but that we should not *neglect* prayer, and that we should *ever be in a prayerful frame of mind,* even when walking by the way or engaged in the duties of life—ever ready to send up our petitions to heaven for help in time of need.

Preparation for Christ's Return

That we might be prepared for His coming, what admonition did Christ give?

"*Take heed, watch and pray;* for you do not know when the time is. . . . And what I say to you, I say to all: *Watch!*" Mark 13:33-37. (See also Luke 21:36.)

Why are watchfulness and prayer especially imperative in the last days?

"Woe to the inhabitants of the earth and the sea! For the devil has come down to you, having great wrath, because he knows that he has a short time." Revelation 12:12.

God's Unlimited Ability

How does God anticipate the needs of His children?

"It shall come to pass that *before they call, I will answer; and while they are still speaking, I will hear.*" Isaiah 65:24.

Is there any limit to God's ability to help?

"Now to Him who is *able to do exceedingly abundantly above all that we ask or think,* according to the power that works in us." Ephesians 3:20.

How fully has God promised to supply our needs?

"And my God *shall supply all your need* according to His riches in glory by Christ Jesus." Philippians 4:19.

Our Limited Understanding

Do we always know what to pray for?

"Likewise the Spirit also helps in our weaknesses. For *we do not know what we should pray for as we ought.*" Romans 8:26.

Does God always see fit to grant our petitions?

"Concerning this thing I pleaded with the Lord three times that it might depart from me. And He said to me, 'My grace is sufficient for you, for My strength is made perfect in weakness.'" 2 Corinthians 12:8, 9.

NOTE—Paul's affliction, some have thought, was impaired sight. (See Acts 9:8, 9, 18; 22:11-13.) The retaining of such an imperfection would be a constant reminder to him of his conversion, and hence a blessing in disguise.

Patience and Perseverance

If an answer does not come at once, what should we do?

"Rest in the Lord, and *wait patiently for Him.*" Psalm 37:7.

Why was the parable of the importunate widow given?

"Then He spoke a parable to them, *that men always ought to pray and not lose heart.*" Luke 18:1.

NOTE—The request of the importunate widow was granted because of her persistency. God wants us to *seek* Him *earnestly,* when we pray. He is a rewarder of them that *diligently* seek Him. (Hebrews 11:6.)

How did Elijah pray before obtaining his request?

"Elijah was a man with a nature like ours, and *he prayed earnestly* that it would not rain; and it did not rain on the land for three years and six months. And he prayed again, and the heaven gave rain, and the earth produced its fruit." James 5:17, 18. (See Revelation 11:3-6.)

Two Fundamental Conditions

Upon what condition does Christ say we shall receive?

"Therefore I say to you, whatever things you ask when you pray, *believe that you receive them, and you will have them.*" Mark 11:24.

Without this faith, will God answer prayer?

"*But let him ask in faith, with no doubting,* for he who doubts is like a wave of the sea driven and tossed by the wind. *For let not that man suppose that he will receive anything from the Lord.*" James 1:6, 7.

What petitions may we confidently expect God to hear?

"Now this is the confidence that we have in Him, that *if we ask anything according to His will,* He hears us. And if we know that He hears us, whatever we ask, we know that we have the petitions that we have asked of Him." 1 John 5:14, 15.

NOTE—God's will is expressed in His law, His promises, and His Word. (Psalm 40:8; Romans 2:17, 18; 1 Peter 1:4.)

Examples of Answered Prayer

When Daniel and his fellows were about to be slain because the wise men of Babylon could not reveal Nebuchadnezzar's dream to him, how did God answer their united prayers?

"*Then the secret was revealed to Daniel in a night vision.* So Daniel blessed the God of heaven." Daniel 2:19.

NOTE—In 1839 the sultan of Turkey decreed that not a representative of the Christian religion should remain in the empire. Learning of this, William Goodell, an American missionary to Turkey, came home to his friend and colleague, Cyrus Hamlin, the first president of Robert College, Constantinople, with the sad news: "It is all over with us; we have to leave. The American consul and the

Bible Answers

but thought he was seeing a vision. When they were past the first and the second guard posts, they came to the iron gate that leads to the city, which opened to them of its own accord; and they went out and went down one street, and immediately the angel departed from him." Verses 7-10.

Because Solomon asked for wisdom rather than for long life and riches, what besides wisdom did God give him?

"Because you have asked this thing, behold, I have done according to your words; see, I have given you a wise and understanding heart. . . . And I have also given you what you have not asked: *both riches and honor.*" 1 Kings 3:11-13.

NOTE—The following are some things we are taught in the Scriptures to pray for: (1) For daily bread. Matthew 6:11. (2) For the forgiveness of sin. 2 Chronicles 7:14; Psalm 32:5, 6; 1 John 1:9; 5:16. (3) For the Holy Spirit. Luke 11:13; Zechariah 10:1; John 14:16. (4) For deliverance in the hour of temptation and danger. Matthew 6:13; John 17:11, 15; Proverbs 3:26; Psalm 91; Matthew 24:20. (5) For wisdom and understanding. James 1:5; 1 Kings 3:9; Daniel 2:17-19. (6) For peaceable and quiet lives. 1 Timothy 2:1, 2. (7) For the healing of the sick. James 5:14, 15; 2 Kings 20:1-11. (8) For the prosperity of the ministers of God and the gospel. Ephesians 6:18, 19; Colossians 4:3; 2 Thessalonians 3:1. (9) For those who suffer for the truth's sake. Hebrews 13:3; Acts 12:5. (10) For kings, rulers, and all in authority. 1 Timothy 2:1, 2; Ezra 6:10. (11) For temporal prosperity. 2 Corinthians 9:10; James 5:17, 18. (12) For our enemies. Matthew 5:44. (13) For all saints. Ephesians 6:18. (14) For all men. 1 Timothy 2:1. (15) For the Lord to vindicate His cause. 1 Kings 18:30-39. (16) For the coming of Christ and of God's kingdom. Matthew 6:10; Revelation 22:20.

British ambassador say it is no use to meet with antagonism this violent and vindictive monarch." To this Hamlin replied: "The sultan of the universe can, in answer to prayer, change the decree of the sultan of Turkey." They gave themselves to prayer. The next day the sultan died, and the decree was never executed. (See Daniel 4:17, 24, 25.)

When Peter was imprisoned and about to be executed by Herod, what did the church do?

"Peter was therefore kept in prison, but *constant prayer was offered to God for him by the church.*" Acts 12:5.

How were their prayers answered?

"Behold, an angel of the Lord stood by him, and a light shone in the prison; and he struck Peter on the side and raised him up, saying, 'Arise quickly!' And his chains fell off his hands. Then the angel said to him, 'Gird yourself and tie on your sandals'; and so he did. And he said to him, 'Put on your garment and follow me.' So he went out and followed him, and did not know that what was done by the angel was real,

Chapter 20

The Good News About
God's People

A Woman Clothed With the Sun

Under what figure was the Christian church represented to the apostle John?

"Now a great sign appeared in heaven: *a woman* clothed with the sun, with the moon under her feet, and on her head a garland of twelve stars." Revelation 12:1.

NOTE—Frequently in the Scriptures a woman is used to represent the church. (See Jeremiah 6:2; 2 Corinthians 11:2.) The sun represents the light of the gospel with which the church was clothed at the first advent (1 John 2:8); the moon under her feet, the waning light of the former dispensation; and the 12 stars, the 12 apostles.

How is the church at the First Advent described?

"Then being with child, she cried out in labor and in pain to give birth." Revelation 12:2.

NOTE—The church is in labor and pain while she brings forth Christ and her children, in the midst of afflictions and persecutions. (See Romans 8:19, 22; 1 John 3:1, 2; 2 Timothy 3:12.)

How are the birth, work, and ascension of Christ briefly described?

"She bore a male Child who was to rule all nations with a rod of iron. And her Child was caught up to God and His throne." Revelation 12:5.

NOTE—That this passage refers to Christ is clearly evident when it is compared with Psalm 2:7-9.

The Great Red Dragon

What other sign, or wonder, appeared in heaven?

"And another sign appeared in heaven: behold, *a great, fiery red dragon* having seven heads and ten horns, and seven diadems on his heads. His tail drew a third of the stars of heaven and threw them to the earth. And the dragon stood before the woman who was ready to give birth, to devour her

Child as soon as it was born." Revelation 12:3, 4.

Who is this dragon said to be?

"So the great dragon was cast out, *that serpent of old,* called the *Devil* and *Satan,* who deceives the whole world." Verse 9.

NOTE—Primarily the dragon represents Satan, the great enemy and persecutor of the church in all ages. But Satan works through principalities and powers in his efforts to destroy the people of God. It was through a Roman king, King Herod, that he sought to destroy Christ as soon as He was born. (Matthew 2:16.) Rome must therefore also be symbolized by the dragon. The seven heads of the dragon are interpreted by some to refer to the "seven hills" upon which the city of Rome is built; by others, to the seven forms of government through which Rome passed; and by still others, and more broadly, to the seven great monarchies which have oppressed the people of God, namely, Egypt, Assyria, Chaldea, Persia, Greece, pagan Rome, and papal Rome, in either of which Rome is represented and included. (See pages 86-88.) The 10 horns, as in the fourth beast of Daniel 7, evidently refer to the kingdoms into which Rome was finally divided, and thus again identify the dragon with the Roman power.

How is the conflict in heaven described?

"And war broke out in heaven: Michael and his angels fought with the dragon; and the dragon and his angels fought, but they did not prevail, nor was a place found for them in heaven any longer. So the great dragon was cast out, that serpent of old, called the Devil and Satan, who deceives the whole world; he was cast to the earth, and his angels were cast out with him." Revelation 12:7-9.

NOTE—This conflict, begun in heaven, continues on earth. Near the close of Christ's ministry He said, "I saw Satan fall like lightning from heaven." Luke 10:18. "Now is the judgment of this world; now the ruler of this world will be *cast out.*" John 12:31. From the councils of the representatives of the various worlds to which Satan, as the prince of this world, was formerly admitted (Job 1:6, 7; 2:1, 2), he was cast out when he crucified Christ.

Bible Answers

What shout of triumph was heard in heaven following the victory gained by Christ?

"Then I heard a loud voice saying in heaven, 'Now salvation, and strength, and the kingdom of our God, and the power of His Christ have come, for the accuser of our brethren, who accused them before our God day and night." Revelation 12:10.

Persecution on Earth

Why was woe at this time proclaimed to the world?

"Woe to the inhabitants of the earth and the sea! *For the devil has come down to you, having great wrath, because he knows that he has a short time.*" Verse 12.

NOTE—This shows that, since the crucifixion of Christ, Satan knows that his doom is sealed and that he has but a limited time in which to work, also that his efforts are now largely if not wholly confined to this world and concentrated upon its inhabitants.

What did the dragon do when cast to the earth?

"Now when the dragon saw that he had been cast to the earth, *he persecuted the woman* who gave birth to the male Child." Verse 13.

NOTE—The persecution of Christians began under pagan Rome, but was carried on far more extensively under papal Rome. (See Matthew 24:21, 22.)

What period of time was allotted to this great persecution of God's people under papal Rome?

"But the woman was given two wings of a great eagle, that she might fly into the wilderness to her place, where she is nourished for *a time and times and half a time,* from the presence of the serpent." Revelation 12:14.

NOTE—This is the same period as that of Daniel 7:25, and, like the 10 horns, identifies the dragon with the fourth beast of Daniel 7, and its later work with the work of the little horn of that same beast. In Revelation 13:5 this period is referred to as "forty-two months," in Revelation 12:6 as 1260 days, each representing 1260 literal years, the period allotted to the supremacy of papal Rome. Beginning in A.D. 538, it ended in 1798, when the pope was taken prisoner by the French. The woman fleeing into the wilderness fittingly describes the condition of the church during those times of bitter persecution.

What was Satan's plan in persecuting the church?

"So the serpent spewed water out of his mouth like a flood after the woman, *that he might cause her to be carried away by the flood.*" Revelation 12:15.

How was the flood stayed, and Satan defeated?

"But *the earth helped the woman,* and the earth opened its mouth and swallowed up the flood which the dragon had spewed out of his mouth." Verse 16.

NOTE—The mountain fastnesses, quiet retreats, and secluded valleys of Europe for centuries shielded many who refused allegiance to the Papacy. Here, too, may be seen the results of the work of the Reformation of the sixteenth century, when some of the governments of Europe came to the help of various reform groups by staying the hand of persecution and protecting the lives of those who dared to take their stand against the Papacy. The discovery of America and the opening up of this country as an asylum for the oppressed of Europe at this time may also be included in the "help" here referred to.

What did Christ say would be the result if the days of persecution were not shortened?

"And unless those days were shortened, *no flesh would be saved;* but for the elect's sake those days will be shortened." Matthew 24:22.

How does Satan manifest his enmity against the remnant church?

"And the dragon was enraged with the woman, and *he went to make war with the rest of her offspring,* who keep the commandments of God and have the testimony of Jesus Christ." Revelation 12:17.

A Warning Against False Worship

What indicates that the messages of the judgment hour and the fall of Babylon are two parts of a threefold message?

"Then *a third angel followed them.*" Revelation 14:9.

What apostasy from the worship of God is named here?

"If anyone *worships the beast and his image, and receives his mark* on his forehead or on his hand." Verse 9.

What is to be the fate of those who, instead of worshipping God, engage in this false worship?

"*He himself shall also drink of the wine of the wrath of God, which is poured out full strength into the cup of His indignation. He shall be tormented with fire and brimstone in the presence of the holy angels and in the presence of the Lamb. And the smoke of their torment ascends forever and ever; and they have no rest day or night, who worship the beast and his image, and whoever receives the mark of his name." Verses 10, 11. (See Isaiah 33:13; 34:1-10; Hebrews 12:29.)

How are those who heed this warning described?

"Here is the patience of the saints; here are those who keep the commandments of God and the faith of Jesus." Revelation 14:12.

Who Is the Beast Power?

What description is given of the beast against whose worship this closing warning message is given?

"Then I stood on the sand of the sea. And I saw a beast rising up out of the sea, having seven heads and ten horns, and on his horns ten crowns, and on his heads a blasphemous name. Now the beast which I saw was like a leopard, his feet were like the feet of a bear, and his mouth like the mouth of a lion. The dragon gave him his power, his throne, and great authority." Revelation 13:1, 2.

NOTE—In this composite beast from the sea are combined the symbols of the seventh chapter of Daniel, representing the Roman, Greco-Macedonian, Medio-Persian, and the Babylonian empires. Its blasphemous words, its persecution of the saints, and its allotted time (Revelation 13:5-7) show that this beast, under one of its seven-headed manifestations, is identical with the little horn of the vision of Daniel 7, modern Babylon, the Papacy. The worship of the beast is the rendering of that homage to the Papacy that is due God alone. The system of religion enforced by the Papacy contains the paganism of Babylon, Persia, Greece, and Rome, indicated by the beast's composite character (Revelation 13:2), disguised under the forms and names of Christianity. The Roman Pontifex Maximus, for instance, was continued in the pope, who is the head of the Roman priesthood. But this scripture in Revelation shows that the pope's power and his seat and his great authority do not come from Christ.

What challenge is made by those who worship the beast?

"So they worshiped the dragon who gave authority to the beast; and they worshiped the beast, saying, '*Who is like the beast? Who is able to make war with him?*'" Verse 4.

Whose sovereignty is thus challenged?

"Inasmuch as *there is none like You, O Lord* (You are great, and Your name is great in might)." Jeremiah 10:6. (See Psalms 71:19; 86:8; 89:6, 8.)

What specifications of "the man of sin" are thus met?

"Let no one deceive you by any means; for that Day will not come unless the falling away comes first, and the man of sin is revealed, the son of perdition, *who opposes and exalts himself above all that is called God or that is worshiped, so that he sits as God in the temple of God, showing himself that he is God.*" 2 Thessalonians 2:3, 4.

What did Babylon give the nations to drink?

"*She has made all nations drink of the wine of the wrath of her fornication.*" Revelation 14:8.

What are those who accept the teachings of Babylon, and thus render homage to the beast, to drink?

"He himself shall also drink of *the wine of the wrath of God,* which is poured out full strength into the cup of His indignation." Verse 10.

NOTE—The cup of the Lord, which contains the new covenant in the blood of Christ, and the cup of the wine of the wrath of Babylon are both offered to the world. To drink of the former, that is, to accept the true gospel, is to receive everlasting life; but to drink of the wine of Babylon, that is, to accept the false gospel taught by the Papacy, will result in drinking of the wine of the wrath of God from the cup of His indignation. The true gospel means everlasting life; the false gospel, everlasting death.

False Worship Enforced

Under what threatened penalty is the worship of the image of the beast enforced?

"He was granted power to give breath to the image of the beast, that the image of the beast should both speak and *cause* [decree] as *many as would not worship the image of the beast to be killed.*" Revelation 13:15.

NOTE—For an explanation of the image of the beast, see "The Dragon's Voice Heard Again," page 86.

What universal boycott is to be employed in an attempt to compel all to receive the mark of the beast?

"He causes all, both small and great, rich and poor, free and slave, to receive a mark on their right hand or on their foreheads, and *that no one may buy or sell except one who has the mark or the name of the beast, or the number of his name.*" Verses 16, 17.

NOTE—Regarding the mark of the beast, see "Sunday Law Advocates," page 87.

Bible Answers

Satan, or God?

Who is the real power operating through the beast?

"Now the beast which I saw was like a leopard, his feet were like the feet of a bear, and his mouth like the mouth of a lion. The *dragon* gave him his power, his throne, and great authority." Verse 2.

Who is this dragon?

"So the great dragon was cast out, that serpent of old, called the *Devil* and *Satan*, who deceives the whole world; he was cast to the earth, and his angels were cast out with him." Revelation 12:9.

How did the devil seek to induce Jesus to worship him?

"Then the devil, taking Him up on a high mountain, showed Him all the kingdoms of the world in a moment of time. And the devil said to Him, '*All this authority I will give You,* and their glory; for this has been delivered to me, and I give it to whomever I wish. *Therefore, if You will worship before me, all will be Yours.*'" Luke 4:5-7.

How did Jesus show His loyalty to God?

"And Jesus answered and said to him, '*Get behind Me, Satan! For it is written, "You shall worship the Lord your God, and Him only you shall serve."*'" Verse 8.

NOTE—The threefold message of Revelation 14:6-12 is proclaimed in connection with the closing scenes of the great controversy between Christ and Satan. Lucifer has sought to put himself in the place of God (Isaiah 14:12-14), and to secure to himself the worship that is due God alone. The final test comes over the commandments of God. Those who acknowledge the supremacy of the beast by yielding obedience to the law of God as changed and enforced by the Papacy, when the real issue has been clearly defined, will, in so doing, worship the beast and his image, and receive his mark. Such will take the side of Satan in his rebellion against God's authority.

The 10-horned Beast of Revelation 13

What is the first symbol of Revelation 13?

"Then I stood on the sand of the sea. And I saw *a beast rising up out of the sea, having seven heads and ten horns,* and on his horns ten crowns, and on his heads a blasphemous name." Verse 1.

NOTE—As already learned from studying the book of Daniel, a beast in prophecy represents some great earthly power or kingdom; a head or horn, a governing power; waters, "peoples, multitudes, nations, and tongues." (Revelation 17:15.)

"The beasts of Daniel and John are empires. The 10-horned beast is the Roman power. . . . The head is the governing power in the body. The heads of this beast represent successive governments."—H. Gratan Guinness, *Romanism and the Reformation,* pp. 144, 145.

How is this beast further described?

"Now the beast which I saw was *like a leopard,* his feet were like the *feet of a bear,* and his mouth like *the mouth of a lion.*" Revelation 13:2.

NOTE—These are the characteristics of the first three symbols of Daniel 7—the *lion, bear,* and *leopard* there representing the kingdoms of *Babylon, Persia,* and *Greece*—and suggest this beast as representing or belonging to the kingdom symbolized by the *fourth beast* of Daniel 7, or *Rome.* Both have 10 horns. Like the dragon of Revelation 12, it also has seven heads; but as the dragon symbolized Rome in its entirety, particularly in its pagan phase, this, like the "little horn" coming up among the 10 horns of the fourth beast of Daniel 7, represents Rome in its later or papal form. Both it and the little horn have "a mouth" speaking great things; both make war upon the saints; both continue for the same period.

Allowing a very broad meaning to the symbol, the Douay Version, or English Catholic Bible, in a note on Revelation 13:1, explains the seven heads of this beast as follows: "The seven heads are seven kings, that is, seven principal kingdoms or empires, which have exercised, or shall exercise, tyrannical power over the people of God: of these, five were then fallen, viz., the Egyptian, Assyrian, Chaldean, Persian, and Grecian monarchies; one was present, viz., the empire of Rome; and the seventh and chiefest was to come, viz., the great Antichrist and his empire." That the seventh head represents antichrist, or the Papacy, there can be little doubt.

The Dragon Gives Place to the Beast

What did the dragon give this beast?

"The dragon gave him his *power,* his *throne,* and *great authority.*" Revelation 13:2.

NOTE—"It is an undisputed fact of history that under the later Roman emperors, after Constantine, the religion of the Roman government was changed from pagan to papal; that the bishops of Rome received rich gifts and great authority from Constantine and succeeding emperors; that after A.D. 476 the bishop of Rome became the most influential power in western Rome, and by Justinian, in 533, was declared 'head of all the holy churches,' and 'corrector of heretics.' The removal of the capital of the Empire from Rome to Constantinople in 330 left the western church, practically free from imperial power, to develop its own form of organization. The bishop of Rome, *in the seat of the Caesars,* was now the greatest man in the West, and was soon [when the barbarians overran the empire] forced to become the political as well as the spiritual head."—A. C. Flick, *The Rise of the Mediaeval Church* (Putnam's, 1909 ed.), p. 168. (Italics supplied.)

Thus Rome pagan became Rome papal; church and state were united, and the persecuting power of the dragon was conferred upon the professed head of the church of Christ, or papal Rome. "The Pope, who calls himself 'King' and 'Pontifex Maximus,' is Caesar's successor."—Adolph Harnack, *What Is Christianity?* (Putnam's, 1903 ed.), p. 270.

How are the character, work, period of supremacy, and great power of the beast described?

"And he was given a mouth speaking great things and blasphemies, and he was given authority to continue for forty-two months. Then he opened his mouth in blasphemy against God, to blaspheme His name, His tabernacle, and those who dwell in heaven. It was granted to him to make war with the saints and to overcome them. And authority was given him over every tribe, tongue, and nation." Verses 5-7.

NOTE—All these specifications have been fully and accurately met in the Papacy, and identify this beast as representing the same power as the represented by the little-horn phase of the fourth beast of Daniel 7, and the little horn of Daniel 8, in its chief and essential features and work. (See Daniel 7:25; 8:11, 12, 24, 25, and readings on pages 46, 47, 82, and 83. For an explanation of the time period mentioned, see page 82.)

The Beast Receives a Deadly Wound

What was to happen to one of the heads of this beast?

"And I saw *one of his heads as if it had been mortally wounded,* and his deadly wound was healed. And all the world marveled and followed the beast." Revelation 13:3.

NOTE—The "deadly wound" to the papal head of this beast was inflicted when the French, in 1798, entered Rome and took the pope prisoner, eclipsing, for a time, the power of the Papacy and depriving it of its temporalities. Again in 1870 temporal dominion was taken from the Papacy, and the pope looked upon himself as the prisoner of the Vatican. By 1929 the situation had changed to the extent that Cardinal Gasparri met Premier Mussolini in the historic palace of Saint John Lateran to settle a long quarrel—returning temporal power to the Papacy, to "heal a wound of 59

years" *(The Catholic Advocate* [Australia], Apr. 18, 1929, p. 16).

The front page of the San Francisco *Chronicle* of February 12, 1929, carried pictures of Cardinal Gasparri and Mussolini, signers of the Concordat, with the headline "Heal Wound of Many Years." The Associated Press dispatch said: "In affixing the autographs to the memorable document, healing the wound which was festered since 1870, extreme cordiality was displayed on both sides." To such a position of influence over the nations is the Papacy finally to attain that just before her complete overthrow and destruction she will say, "I sit as queen, and am no widow, and will not see sorrow." Revelation 18:7. (See Isaiah 47:7-15; Revelation 17:18.)

What is said of the Papacy's captivity and downfall?

"He who leads into captivity shall go into captivity; he who kills with the sword must be killed with the sword." Revelation 13:10.

What questions indicate the high position of this beast-power?

"So they worshiped the dragon who gave authority to the beast; and they worshiped the beast, saying, 'Who is like the beast? Who is able to make war with him?'" Verse 4.

How universal is the worship of this power to become?

"All who dwell on the earth will worship him, whose names have not been written in the Book of Life of the Lamb slain from the foundation of the world." Verse 8.

The Beast Destroyed

What did John say was to be the end of this beast?

"Then the beast was captured, and with him the false prophet who worked signs in his presence, by which he deceived those who received the mark of the beast and those who worshiped his image. *These two were cast alive into the lake of fire burning with brimstone.*" Revelation 19:20. (See Isaiah 47:7-15; 2 Thessalonians 2:3-8; Revelation 17:16, 17; 18:4-8.)

What is the fate of the fourth beast of Daniel 7?

"I watched then because of the sound of the pompous words which the horn was speaking; I watched till the beast was *slain,* and its body *destroyed* and *given to the burning flame.*" Verse 11.

Another Beast Appears

When was the papal head of the first beast of Revelation 13 wounded?

Bible Answers

In 1798, when the Papacy was temporarily overthrown by the French, under General Berthier. (See page 85.)

What did the prophet see coming up at this time?

"Then I saw *another beast coming up out of the earth,* and he had two horns like a lamb and spoke like a dragon." Revelation 13:11.

NOTE—John Wesley, in his note on Revelation 13:11, written in 1754, says of the two-horned beast: "He is not yet come: tho' he cannot be far off. For he is to appear at the End of the forty-two Months of the first Beast."—*Explanatory Notes Upon the New Testament* (1791 ed.), vol. 3, p. 299.

The previous beast came up out of the "sea," which indicates its rise among the peoples and nations of the world then in existence (Revelation 17:15), whereas this latter power comes up out of the "earth," where there had not before been "peoples, and multitudes, and nations, and tongues." In 1798, when the papal power received its deadly wound, the United States, located in the Western Hemisphere, was the only great world power then coming into prominence in territory not previously occupied by peoples, multitudes, and nations. Only nine years preceding this (in 1789), the United States adopted its national Constitution. It is within the territory of the United States, therefore, that we may look for a fulfillment of this prophecy.

The eminent American preacher De Witt Talmage based a sermon, "America for God," on the text of Revelation 13:11, interpreting the beast with two horns like a lamb as referring to the United States. "Is it reasonable," he said, "to suppose that God would leave out from the prophecies of his Book this whole Western Hemisphere? No, No!" See his *500 Selected Sermons* (1900), vol. 2, p. 9.

What is the character of this new power?

"He had *two horns like a lamb.*" Verse 11.

NOTE—How fittingly is the United States characterized in these words! The nations of the past, pictured in the Bible as beasts of prey, were filled with intolerance, persecution, and oppression. In sharp contrast, the United States was founded on the principles of liberty, equality, and tolerance. Those who had fled the tribulations of the Old World were determined that those trials should not be repeated in the New.

The principles of civil and religious liberty that have made the United States great were incorporated into the fundamental law of the nation at its very founding. We quote from the first amendments to the Constitution, commonly known as the Bill of Rights:

Article I. "Congress shall make no law respecting an establishment of religion, or prohibiting the free exercise thereof; or abridging the freedom of speech or of the press; or the right of the people peaceably to assemble, and to petition the government for a redress of grievances."

Article IV. "The right of the people to be secure in their persons, houses, papers, and effects, against unreasonable searches and seizures, shall not be violated."

Article V. "No person shall be . . . subject for the same offense to be twice put in jeopardy of life or limb, nor shall be compelled in any criminal case to be a witness against himself; nor to be deprived of life, liberty, or property, without due process of law; nor shall private property be taken for public use without just compensation."

For these principles many have fought and died. For them leaders of the people have valiantly contended throughout the nation's history. For these liberties, millions today are ready to sacrifice even life itself.

The Dragon's Voice Heard Again

Notwithstanding the lamblike appearance of this power, what will ultimately happen?

"And he . . . *spoke like a dragon.*" Verse 11.

NOTE—The voice of the dragon is the voice of intolerance and persecution. It is repugnant to the American mind to think that religious persecution might mar the fair record of the nation founded on liberty to all. But all through the history of the country, from its very founding, farseeing leaders have recognized that the tendency to enforce religious dogmas by civil law is all too common with humaniaty, and is likely to break out in active persecution in unexpected places unless specifically guarded against.

Said Thomas Jefferson, at the very beginning of the nation's existence: "The spirit of the times may alter, will alter. Our rulers will become corrupt, our people careless. A single zealot may commence persecution, and better men be his victims."—*Notes on Virginia,* Query XVII, in *The Works of Thomas Jefferson* (Ford ed., 1904-1905), vol. 4, pp. 81, 82.

In a letter to Rabbi Mordecai M. Noah, this same great American wrote: "Your sect by its sufferings has furnished a remarkable proof of the universal spirit of religious intolerance, inherent in every sect. . . . Our laws have applied the only antidote to the vice. . . . But more remains to be done; for although we are free by the law, we are not so in practice; public opinion erects itself into an Inquisition, and exercises its office with as much fanaticism as fans the flames of an auto da fe."—Letter to Mordecai M. Noah, May 28, 1818, *Thomas Jefferson Paper,* vol. 213, p. 37988, in Manuscript Division, Library of Congress.

To the honor of the nation, it should be said that

noble leaders have largely held in check the tendency that Thomas Jefferson foresaw working in the body politic. But no American can ignore the fact that paralleling these noble efforts, zealous efforts have been made by misguided religious leaders to secure civil enforcement of religious usages.

How much power will this beast exercise?

"And *he exercises all the authority of the first beast in his presence,* and causes the earth and those who dwell in it to worship the first beast, whose deadly wound was healed." Verse 12.

NOTE—The "first beast in his presence"—papal Rome (see pages 84, 85)—exercised the power of persecuting all who differed with it in religious matters.

What means will be employed to lead the people back into false worship?

"And he deceives those who dwell on the earth *by those signs which he was granted to do* in the sight of the beast." Verse 14.

What will this power propose that the people shall do?

"Telling those who dwell on the earth to *make an image to the beast who was wounded by the sword and lived.*" Verse 14.

NOTE—The beast "which was wounded by the sword and lived," is the Papacy. That was a church dominating the civil power, a union of church and state, enforcing its religious dogmas by the civil power, by confiscation, imprisonment, and death. An image to this beast would be another ecclesiastical organization clothed with civil power—another union of church and state—to enforce religion by law.

Sunday Law Advocates

Does the history of the United States show that religious organizations have attempted to secure legislation involving religion?

Organizations such as the National Reform Association, the International Reform Federation, the Lord's Day Alliance of the United States, and the New York Sabbath Committee have for years worked to secure Sunday legislation. They have often secured the aid of civic groups.

What, according to its constitution, is an avowed object of the National Reform Association?

"To secure such an amendment to the Constitution of the United States as will . . . indicate that this is a Christian nation, and place all the Christian laws, institutions, and usages of our government on an undeniably legal basis in the fundamental law of the land."—David McAllister, *The National Reform Movement . . . a Manual of Christian Civil Government* (1898 ed.), "Article II of Constitution," pp. 15, 16.

NOTE—A general superintendent of the National Reform Association and editor of the *Christian Statesman* propounded the following amendment to the First Amendment of the United States Constitution:

"How to take a most dangerous weapon out of the hands of secularists: Amend the highest written law of the land, our Federal Constitution, so that it shall plainly proclaim the will of the Lord of nations as the rule of our national life and the standard of our national conduct in dealing with all our problems—internal and external, national and international. As that Constitution now stands, the secularist is perpetually quoting it on his side, loudly proclaiming that there is in it nothing that warrants the Christian usages, and as loudly and persistently demanding that all these and their like shall go out of the latter that it may be brought into perfect harmony with the former. Our answer should be—Never! But we will instead change the written document that it may be in perfect harmony with the unwritten and so furnish an undeniably legal basis for all we have that is Christian in our national life and character and also for more of its kind that is still needed."—*Christian Statesman*, August 1921, p. 25.

At first glance such a statement as this might appear worthy of endorsement. But a closer examination reveals a reasoning basically the same as that employed by religious leaders of past ages, who persecuted all who differed with them. If the laws of the land should regulate religious observances, an individual could be forced to attend church, to be baptized, or to pay for the support of the clergy.

What has this association said on this point regarding the Catholic Church?

"We cordially, gladly, recognize the fact that in South American Republics, and in France and other European countries, the Roman Catholics are the recognized advocates of national Christianity, and stand opposed to all the proposals of secularism.... *Whenever they are willing to cooperate in resisting the progress of political atheism, we will gladly join hands with them* in a World's Conference for the promotion of National Christianity—which ought to be held at no distant day—many countries could be represented only by Roman Catholics."—Editorial, *Christian Statesman* (official organ of the National Reform Association), Dec. 11, 1884, p. 2. (Italics supplied.)

What has the pope commanded all Catholics to do in regard to government?

"First and foremost it is the duty of all Catholics worthy of the name and wishful to be known as the most loving children of the Church . . . to endeavor to bring back all civil society to the pattern and form of Christianity which we have described."—*The Great Encyclical Letters of Leo XIII,* "Encyclical Letter *Immortale Dei*, Nov. 1, 1885," p. 132.

NOTE—On September 7, 1947, Pope Pius XII declared that "'the time for reflection and planning is past' in religious and moral fields and the 'time for action' has arrived." He said that "the battle in religious and moral fields hinged on five points: Religious culture, *the sanctifying of Sunday,* the saving of the Christian family, social justice, and loyalty and truthfulness in dealings."—*Evening Star* (Washington, D.C.), Sept. 8, 1947. (Italics supplied.)

On September 21, 1961, Pope John, in an audience with members of a labor union, asked for the proper observance of Sunday as a day of rest. Said the pope, This "presupposes a change of mind in society and the *intervention of the powers of the state.*"

What is the object of the International Reform Federation?

"The Reform Bureau [now Federation] is the first 'Christian lobby' established at our national capital to speak to government in behalf of all denominations."—*History of the International Reform Bureau* (1911), p. 2.

NOTE—The securing of compulsory Sunday legislation is one of the chief objects of this and other like organizations. (See pages 60-62 of the above-named work.)

What is the object of the Lord's Day Alliance?

"This organization proposes in every possible way to aid in preserving Sunday as a *civil institution.* Our national security requires the active support of all good citizens in the maintenance of our American Sabbath. *Sunday laws must be enacted and enforced.*"—Quoted as "principles contained in the Constitution" of the original organization (then called the American Sabbath Union); cited in *The Lord's Day Alliance, Twenty-fifth Annual Report* (1913), p. 6. (Italics supplied.)

What was one of the first objectives stated by the Federal Council of the Churches of Christ in America (predecessor of the National Council of the Churches of Christ in the United States of America)?

"That all encroachments upon the claims and the sanctities of the Lord's Day should be *stoutly resisted* through the press, the Lord's Day associations and alliances, *and by such legislation as may be secured to protect and preserve this bulwark of our American Christianity.*"—Resolution passed in the first meeting of the Federal Council of the Churches of Christ in America (1908), in its first *Biennial Report,* p. 103. (Italics supplied.)

NOTE—Thus it will be seen that the securing of laws for the enforcement of Sunday observance is a prominent feature in all these organizations in their efforts to "Christianize" the nation. In doing this many fail to see that they are repudiating the principles of Christianity, of Protestantism, and of the United States Constitution, and playing directly into the hand of that power that originated the Sunday sabbath—the Papacy.

What arguments have been offered for Sunday laws?

"That the day might be devoted with less interruption to the purposes of devotion." "That the devotion of the faithful might be free from all disturbance."—Augustus Neander, *General History of the Christian Religion and Church,* Torrey translation (3rd American ed.), vol. 2, p. 301.

NOTE—In the fourth and fifth centuries Sunday shows and Sunday theaters, it was complained, hindered the "devotion of the faithful," because many of the members attended them in preference to the church services. The church, therefore, demanded that the state should interfere and promote Sunday observance by law. "In this way," says Neander, "the church received help from the state for the furtherance of her ends."—*Ibid.,* pp. 300, 301. This union of church and state served to establish the Papacy in power. A similar course pursued now will produce the same results.

"On the baseless assumption that the seventh day, set apart and established in the law, has been in some way superseded by the first day, recognized in the gospel, a good deal of hurtful legislation has been enacted on the pretext of sanctifying the Sabbath and honoring God. Men who really do know better are willing to wrest the Scriptures and appeal to popular ignorance in order to gain a point. Such conduct is unworthy of any good cause.

"This error had its origin in the iniquitous union of church and state, and is a relic of that oppressive system. . . . In current usage the so-called Sabbath legislation does not apply to the Bible Sabbath at all, but to the first day of the week. The practical effect of such legislation generally is to annul the divine commandment, and to put in its place a human statute. The vicious assumption underlying such legislation is that divine law may be changed or amended by human enactment. In thousands of minds today the law of God concerning the Sabbath day is rendered of none effect by the so-called Sabbath legislation enacted by civil governments. Such legislation belittles the authority of Jehovah."—J. J. Taylor (Baptist), *The Sabbatic Question* (New York: Fleming H. Revell, 1914), pp. 51, 52, 58.

Early and Modern Sunday Laws

Who is responsible for the present Sunday laws in the United States?

"During nearly all our American history *the churches* have influenced the States to make and improve Sabbath laws."—W. F. Crafts, in *Christian Statesman,* July 3, 1890, p. 5. (Italics supplied.)

NOTE—These Sunday laws are a survival of the complete union of church and state that existed at the founding of the colonies. "Such laws [as the Maryland Sunday law of 1723] were the outgrowth of the system of religious intolerance that prevailed in many of the colonies."—Decision of Court of Appeals of the District of Columbia, Jan. 21, 1908, in *Washington Law Reporter,* Feb. 14, 1908, p. 103.

The first Sunday law imposed on an American colony (Virginia, 1610) required church attendance and prescribed the death penalty for the third offense. (See Peter Force, *Tracts Relating to the Colonies in North America* [1844 ed.], vol. 3, no. 2, p. 11.)

Why is a national Sunday law demanded?

"National Sunday legislation is needed to make the state laws complete and effective," say its advocates.

NOTE—The *state* laws enforcing a religious day are relics of a union of church and state in colonial times. But the *nation* whose foundation principles of civil and religious freedom are aptly symbolized by two lamblike horns does not exercise "all the power of the first beast" and require people "to worship the first beast, whose deadly wound was healed," until it abandons its separation of church and state to the extent of enforcing religious requirements on a national scale, thus constituting an "image," or likeness, to the first beast.

The Mark of Papal Authority

What does the prophet say this second ecclesiastico-political power will attempt to enforce upon all the people?

"He causes all, both small and great, rich and poor, free and slave, to receive *a mark* on their right hand or on their foreheads." Revelation 13:16.

NOTE—This mark, called in verse 17 "the mark . . . of the beast," is set over against the seal of God in the book of Revelation. (See Revelation 14:9, 10.)

What means will be employed to compel all to receive this mark?

"And *that no one may buy or sell except one who has the mark* or the name of the beast, or the number of his name." Revelation 13:17.

NOTE—That is, all who refuse to receive this mark will be boycotted, or denied the rights and privileges of business and trade, or the ordinary means of gaining a livelihood.

Chapter 21

The Good News About
Financial Security

God's Portion and Its Purpose

What is one way in which we are commanded to honor God?

"Honor the Lord *with your possessions,* and *with the firstfruits of all your increase.*" Proverbs 3:9.

What part of one's income has the Lord especially claimed as His?

"And *all the tithe [tenth] of the land,* whether of the seed of the land or of the fruit of the tree, *is the Lord's. It is holy to the Lord.*" Leviticus 27:30.

For whose support and for what work was the tithe devoted in Israel?

"Behold, I have given *the children of Levi* all the tithes in Israel as an inheritance in return *for the work which they perform, the work of the tabernacle of meeting.*" Numbers 18:21.

How does Paul say gospel ministry is supported?

"If we have sown spiritual things for you, is it a great thing if we reap your material things? . . . Do you not know that those who minister the holy things eat of the things of the temple, and those who serve at the altar partake of the offerings of the altar? *Even so the Lord has commanded that those who preach the gospel should live from the gospel.*" 1 Corinthians 9:11-14.

Fundamental Basis of Tithe Paying

Upon what fundamental basis does the requirement of tithe paying rest?

"*The earth is the Lord's,* and all its fullness, the world and those who dwell therein." Psalm 24:1.

Who is it that gives humans power to get wealth on earth?

"And you shall remember the Lord your God, for *it is He who gives you power to get wealth.*" Deuteronomy 8:18.

What statement of Christ's shows that humans are not original owners, but stewards of God's goods?

"For the kingdom of heaven is like a man traveling to a far country, who called his own servants and *delivered his goods to them.*" Matthew 25:14. (See 1 Corinthians 4:7.)

History of Tithe Paying

How early in the history of the world do we read of tithe paying?

"For this Melchizedek, king of Salem, priest of the Most High God, who met Abraham returning from the slaughter of the kings and blessed him, to whom also *Abraham gave a tenth part of all.*" Hebrews 7:1, 2. (See Genesis 14:17-20.)

What vow did Jacob make at Bethel?

"Then Jacob made a vow, saying, 'If God will be with me, and keep me in this way that I am going, and give me bread to eat and clothing to put on, so that I come back to my father's house in peace, then the Lord shall be my God. . . . And *of all that You give me I will surely give a tenth to You.*'" Genesis 28:20-22.

Curse or Blessing

Of what is one who withholds the tithe and freewill offerings guilty?

"Will a man rob God? Yet *you have robbed Me!* But you say, 'In what way have we robbed You?' *In tithes and offerings.*" Malachi 3:8.

Concerning what does the Lord ask us to prove Him, and upon what conditions does He promise great blessings?

"'*Bring all the tithes into the storehouse,* that there may be food in My house, and *try Me now in this,*' says the Lord of hosts, 'if I will not open for you the windows of heaven and pour out for you such blessing that there will not be room enough to receive it. And I will rebuke the devourer for your sakes, so that he will not destroy the fruit of your ground, nor shall the vine fail to bear fruit for you in the field,' says the Lord of hosts." Verses 10, 11.

A Distinction in Tithes and Offerings

By what has God ordained that His work be sustained?

"Tithes and offerings." Malachi 3:8.

How are we told to come into His courts?

"*Bring an offering,* and come into His courts." Psalm 96:8.

NOTE—Various offerings are mentioned in the Bible, such as thank offerings, peace offerings, sin offerings, and trespass offerings.

Concerning the celebration of the three annual feasts, what instruction did God give to His people anciently?

"Three times you shall keep a feast to Me in the year.... *None shall appear before Me empty.*" Exodus 23:14, 15.

Acceptable Offerings

With what spirit would God have us give?

"So let each one give as he purposes in his heart, not grudgingly or of necessity; for *God loves a cheerful giver.*" 2 Corinthians 9:7.

What has Christ said regarding giving?

"*It is more blessed to give than to receive.*" Acts 20:35.

According to what rule were the Israelites commanded to give?

"*Every man shall give as he is able,* according to the blessing of the Lord your God which He has given you." Deuteronomy 16:17. (Compare 1 Corinthians 16:2.)

Upon what basis are gifts acceptable to God?

"For if there is first a willing mind, *it is accepted according to what one has,* and not according to what he does not have." 2 Corinthians 8:12.

What charge was Timothy instructed to give the rich?

"Command those who are rich in this present age not to be haughty, nor to trust in uncertain riches but in the living God, who gives us richly all things to enjoy. *Let them do good, that they be rich in good works, ready to give, willing to share,* storing up for themselves a good foundation for the time to come, that they may lay hold on eternal life." 1 Timothy 6:17-19.

How does God regard such a course?

"But do not forget to do good and to share ["share what you have," RSV], for *with such sacrifices God is well pleased.*" Hebrews 13:16.

The Case of the Covetous

How does God regard the covetous?

"For the wicked boasts of his heart's desire; He blesses the greedy and renounces the Lord." Psalm 10:3. (See Exodus 18:21.)

What warning did Christ give against covetousness?

"Take heed and *beware of covetousness,* for one's life does not consist in the abundance of the things he possesses." Luke 12:15.

How, in the parable, did God regard the selfish rich person?

"But God said to him, '*Fool!* This night your soul will be required of you; then whose will those things be which you have provided?'" Verse 20.

What application does Christ make of this parable?

"So is he who lays up treasure for himself, and is not rich toward God." Verse 21. (See 1 Timothy 6:7.)

Laying Up Treasures in Heaven

By what means can individuals lay up treasure in heaven?

"Sell what you have and give alms; provide yourselves money bags which do not grow old, a treasure in the heavens that does not fail, where no thief approaches nor moth destroys." Luke 12:33. (See 1 Timothy 6:7.)

What indicates where our hearts are?

"For *where your treasure is,* there your heart will be also." Luke 12:34.

Chapter 22

The Good News About
Vibrant Health

What did the apostle John wish concerning Gaius?

"Beloved, I pray *that you may prosper in all things and be in health,* just as your soul prospers." 3 John 2.

What did God promise His people anciently?

"So you shall serve the Lord your God, and He will bless your bread and your water. And *I will take sickness away from the midst of you.*" Exodus 23:25.

Upon what conditions was freedom from disease promised?

"*If you diligently heed the voice of the Lord your God and do what is right in His sight, give ear to His commandments and keep all His statutes,* I will put none of the diseases on you which I have brought on the Egyptians. For I am the Lord who heals you." Exodus 15:26.

What does the psalmist say the Lord does for His people?

"Who forgives all your iniquities, *who heals all your diseases.*" Psalm 103:3.

What constituted a large part of Christ's ministry?

"Who went about doing good and *healing all who were oppressed by the devil,* for God was with Him." Acts 10:38. (See Luke 13:16.) "And Jesus went about all Galilee, . . . *healing all kinds of sickness and all kinds of disease among the people.*" Matthew 4:23.

The Bible Speaks of Our Bodies

Why should the health of the body be preserved?

"For you were bought at a price; therefore *glorify God in your body* and in your spirit, which are God's." 1 Corinthians 6:20.

What is the body of the believer said to be?

"Or do you not know that *your body is the temple of the Holy Spirit* who is in you, whom you have from God, and you are not your own?" Verse 19.

Food Principles—Not Food Fads

What example did Daniel set in this matter?

"But Daniel *purposed in his heart that he would not defile himself with the portion of the king's delicacies, nor with the wine which he drank.*" Daniel 1:8.

With what food did he ask to be provided?

"Please test your servants for ten days, and *let them give us vegetables to eat and water to drink.*" Verse 12.

What was the original diet prescribed for humans?

"And God said, 'See, I have given you *every herb that yields seed* which is on the face of all the earth, and *every tree whose fruit yields seed;* to you it shall be for food.'" Genesis 1:29.

Why did the Lord restrict the Hebrews in their diet?

"*For you are a holy people to the Lord your God, and the Lord has chosen you to be a people for Himself, a special treasure above all the peoples* who are on the face of the earth. You shall not eat any detestable thing." Deuteronomy 14:2, 3.

NOTE—Both mind and body are affected by the food we eat.

Rest, Cheer, and High Purpose

What effect does cheerfulness have upon the health?

"A merry heart *does good,* like medicine." Proverbs 17:22.

How did the Savior provide rest for His disciples?

"And He said to them, 'Come aside by yourselves to a deserted place and *rest a while.*'" Mark 6:31.

How are we exhorted to present our bodies to God?

"I beseech you . . . that *you present your bodies a living sacrifice, holy, acceptable to God.*" Romans 12:1.

What should control our habits of life?

"Therefore, whether you eat or drink, or whatever you do, *do all to the glory of God.*" 1 Corinthians 10:31.

Bible Answers

The Nature and Necessity of Self-control

Concerning what did Paul reason before Felix?

"He reasoned about righteousness, *self-control,* and the judgment to come." Acts 24:25.

NOTE—Self-control means habitual moderation and control in the indulgence of the appetites and passions.

Of what is self-control a fruit?

"But *the fruit of the Spirit* is love, joy, peace, longsuffering, kindness, goodness, faithfulness, gentleness, *self-control.*" Galatians 5:22, 23.

NOTE—"Temperance [self-control] puts wood on the fire, meal in the barrel, flour in the tub, money in the purse, credit in the country, contentment in the house, clothes on the back, and vigor in the body."—Benjamin Franklin.

Where in Christian growth and experience is self-control placed by the apostle Peter?

"Add to your faith virtue, to virtue knowledge, to knowledge self-control, to *self-control* perseverance, to perseverance godliness, to godliness brotherly kindness, and to brotherly kindness love." 2 Peter 1:5-7.

NOTE—Self-control is rightly placed here as to order. Knowledge is a prerequisite to self-control, and self-control to perseverance. It is very difficult for an out-of-control person to persevere.

What is said of those who strive for the mastery?

"And everyone who competes for the prize is *temperate in all things.*" 1 Corinthians 9:25.

The Body and Self-control

In running the Christian race, what did Paul say he did?

"But *I discipline my body and bring it into subjection,* lest, when I have preached to others, I myself should become disqualified." Verse 27.

Why are kings and rulers admonished to have self-control?

"It is not for kings, O Lemuel, it is not for kings to drink wine, nor for princes intoxicating drink; lest they drink and *forget the law, and pervert the justice of all the afflicted.*" Proverbs 31:4, 5.

Why were priests forbidden to use intoxicating drink while engaged in the sanctuary service?

"Then the Lord spoke to Aaron, saying: 'Do not drink wine or intoxicating drink, you, nor your sons with you, when you go into the tabernacle of meeting, lest you die. It shall be a statute forever throughout your generations, *that you may distinguish between holy and unholy, and between unclean and clean.'*" Leviticus 10:8-10.

Why is indulgence in strong drink dangerous?

"And do not be drunk with wine, *in which is dissipation;* but be filled with the Spirit." Ephesians 5:18.

For what should human beings eat and drink?

"Blessed are you, O land, when your king is the son of nobles, and your princes feast at the proper time—*for strength* and not for drunkenness!" Ecclesiastes 10:17.

God's Early Instruction on Diet

What was the original food provided for humans?

"And God said, 'See, I have given you every *herb* that yields *seed* which is on the face of all the earth, and every *tree whose fruit* yields *seed;* to you it shall be for food.'" Genesis 1:29.

NOTE—In other words, vegetables, grains, fruits, and nuts.

After the Flood, what other food was indicated as permissible?

"*Every moving thing that lives* shall be food for you. I have given you all things, even as the green herbs." Genesis 9:3.

NOTE—From this it is evident that flesh food was not included in the original diet provided for humans, but that because of the changed conditions resulting from the Fall and the Flood, its use was permitted. However, Noah understood the difference between the clean and unclean animals, and a larger number of the clean beasts were housed safely in the ark. (See Genesis 7:2.)

Four Fearless Youth Test Self-control

Why did Daniel refuse the food and wine of the king?

"But Daniel purposed in his heart *that he would not defile himself* with the portion of the king's delicacies, nor with the wine which he drank." Daniel 1:8. (See Judges 13:4.)

Instead of these, what did he request?

"Please test your servants for ten days, and let them give us *vegetables to eat* and *water to drink.*" Verse 12.

At the end of the 10 days' test, how did he and his companions appear?

"And at the end of ten days their features appeared *better and fatter in flesh than all the young men who ate the portion of the king's delicacies.*" Verse 15.

At the end of their three years' course in the school of Babylon, how did the wisdom of Daniel and his companions compare with that of others?

"The king interviewed them, *and among them all none was found like Daniel, Hananiah, Mishael, and Azariah.* And in all matters of wisdom and understanding about which the king examined them, *he found them ten times better* than all the magicians and astrologers who were in all his realm." Verses 18-20.

Beginning and End of Drunkards

What warning is given against leading others into intemperance?

"Woe to him who gives drink to his neighbor, pressing him to your bottle, even to make him drunk, that you may look on his nakedness!" Habakkuk 2:15.

What kind of professed Christians are not fellowshipped?

"But now I have written to you not to keep company with anyone named a brother, who is sexually immoral, or covetous, or an idolater, or a reviler, or a *drunkard.*" 1 Corinthians 5:11.

Can drunkards enter the kingdom of God?

"Neither fornicators, nor idolaters, . . . nor thieves, nor covetous, nor *drunkards,* nor revilers, nor extortioners will inherit the kingdom of God." 1 Corinthians 6:9, 10. (See Revelation 21:27.)

For what did Paul pray?

"Now may the God of peace Himself sanctify you completely; and may *your whole spirit, soul, and body be preserved blameless* at the coming of our Lord Jesus Christ." 1 Thessalonians 5:23.

NOTE—For notable examples of total abstinence in the Bible, see the wife of Manoah, the mother of Samson (Judges 13:4, 12-14); Hannah, the mother of Samuel (1 Samuel 1:15); the Rechabites (Jeremiah 35:1-10); and John the Baptist (Luke 1:13-15).

Sacred Admonitions: A Responsive Reading

"*Then the Lord spoke to Aaron, saying: 'Do not drink wine or intoxicating drink, you, nor your sons with you.'*" Leviticus 10:8, 9.

"He who loves pleasure will be a poor man; he who loves wine and oil will not be rich." Proverbs 21:17.

"*For the drunkard and the glutton will come to poverty, and drowsiness will clothe a man with rags.*" Proverbs 23:21.

"Woe to him who gives drink to his neighbor, pressing him to your bottle, even to make him drunk." Habakkuk 2:15.

"*Woe to men mighty at drinking wine, woe to men valiant for mixing intoxicating drink.*" Isaiah 5:22.

"And do not be drunk with wine, in which is dissipation; but be filled with the Spirit." Ephesians 5:18.

"*Wine is a mocker, strong drink is a brawler, and whoever is led astray by it is not wise.*" Proverbs 20:1.

"Who has woe? Who has sorrow? Who has contentions? Who has complaints? Who has wounds without cause? Who has redness of eyes?" Proverbs 23:29.

"*Those who linger long at the wine, those who go in search of mixed wine.*" Verse 30.

"Do not look on the wine when it is red, when it sparkles in the cup, when it swirls around smoothly." Verse 31.

"*At the last it bites like a serpent, and stings like a viper.*" Verse 32.

"Do not be deceived. Neither fornicators, nor idolaters, nor adulterers, . . . nor thieves, nor covetous, nor drunkards, nor revilers, nor extortioners will inherit the kingdom of God." 1 Corinthians 6:9, 10.

"*Now therefore, please be careful not to drink wine or similar drink, and not to eat anything unclean.*" Judges 13:4.

"Or do you not know that your body is the temple of the Holy Spirit who is in you, whom you have from God, and you are not your own?" 1 Corinthians 6:19.

"*For you were bought at a price; therefore glorify God in your body and in your spirit, which are God's.*" Verse 20.

"Therefore, whether you eat or drink, or whatever you do, do all to the glory of God." 1 Corinthians 10:31.

Chapter 23

The Good News About
The Comforter

The Comforter

What precious promise did Jesus make to His disciples shortly before His crucifixion?

"And I will pray the Father, and *He will give you another Helper,* that He may abide with you forever." John 14:16.

Why was it necessary for Christ to go away?

"Nevertheless I tell you the truth. It is to your advantage that I go away; for *if I do not go away, the Helper will not come to you;* but if I depart, I will send Him to you." John 16:7.

Who is the Comforter, and what was He to do?

"But the Helper, the Holy Spirit, whom the Father will send in My name, *He will teach you all things,* and bring to your remembrance all things that I said to you." John 14:26.

What other work was the Comforter to do?

"And when He has come, He will convict [literally, "*convince*"] the world of *sin,* and of *righteousness,* and of *judgment.*" John 16:8.

The Spirit of Truth

By what other title is the Comforter designated?

"But when the Helper comes, whom I shall send to you from the Father, the *Spirit of truth* who proceeds from the Father, He will testify of Me." John 15:26.

What did Jesus say the Spirit of truth would do?

"However, when He, the Spirit of truth, has come, *He will guide you into all truth;* for He will not speak on His own authority, but whatever He hears He will speak; and *He will tell you things to come.*" John 16:13.

NOTE—The Spirit *speaks* (1 Timothy 4:1); *teaches* (1 Corinthians 2:13); *bears witness* (Romans 8:16); *makes intercession* (Romans 8:26); *distributes the gifts* (1 Corinthians 12:11); and *invites the sinner* (Revelation 22:17).

Why cannot the world receive Him?

"The Spirit of truth, whom the world cannot receive, *because it neither sees Him nor knows Him.*" John 14:17.

What did Christ say the Holy Spirit would reveal?

"He will glorify *Me,* for He will take of *what is Mine* and declare it to you." John 16:14.

NOTE—It is plain from these scriptures that the Holy Spirit is the personal representative of Christ upon the earth, abiding in the church by dwelling in the hearts of the believers. It follows that any attempt to make a person the vicegerent of Christ in the place of the third person of the Godhead is an attempt to put a human being in the place of God. Thus does the fundamental principle of the Papacy set aside the person and the work of the Holy Spirit.

How has God revealed to us the hidden things of the kingdom?

"But God has revealed them to us *through His Spirit.* For the Spirit searches all things, yes, the deep things of God." 1 Corinthians 2:10.

Who moved upon the prophets to give their messages?

"For prophecy never came by the will of man, but holy men of God spoke as they were moved by *the Holy Spirit.*" 2 Peter 1:21.

After Pentecost, how was the gospel preached?

"By the Holy Spirit sent from heaven." 1 Peter 1:12.

Heaven's Union With Believers

How intimate is His union with believers?

"But you know Him, for *He dwells with you* and will be in you." John 14:17.

Whose presence does the Holy Spirit bring to the believers?

"I will not leave you orphans; *I will come to you.*" Verse 18.

What promise is thus fulfilled?

"Lo, *I am with you always,* even to the end of the age. Amen." Matthew 28:20. (See also John 14:21-23.)

What threefold union is thus established as the result of belief in Christ?

"At that day you will know that *I am in My Father,* and *you in Me,* and *I in you.*" John 14:20.

NOTE—Romans 8:9 shows the spirit of each of the three persons of the Godhead to be one and the same spirit.

Warning

What warning is therefore given?

"And *do not grieve the Holy Spirit of God,* by whom you were sealed for the day of redemption." Ephesians 4:30.

Is there a limit to the striving of God's Spirit?

"And the Lord said, 'My Spirit shall not strive with man forever.'" Genesis 6:3.

NOTE—The limit is determined by the creature rather than by the Creator. It comes about when there is an utter abandonment to evil, and when further appeals would be without avail. God, foreknowing all things, may designate a definite period of probation for humanity, as in the case of the 120 years before the Flood (Genesis 6:3); but His Spirit never ceases to strive with humans as long as there is hope of their salvation.

For what did David pray?

"Do not cast me away from Your presence, and *do not take Your Holy Spirit from me.*" Psalm 51:11.

Heaven's Willingness and Invitation

How willing is God to give us the Holy Spirit?

"If you then, being evil, know how to give good gifts to your children, how much more will your heavenly Father give the Holy Spirit to those who ask Him!" Luke 11:13.

How does Jesus, through the Spirit, seek an entrance to every heart?

"Behold, *I stand at the door and knock.* If anyone hears My voice and opens the door, I will come in to him and dine with him, and he with Me." Revelation 3:20.

What is the fruit of the Spirit?

"But the fruit of the Spirit is love, joy, peace, longsuffering, kindness, goodness, faithfulness, gentleness, self-control." Galatians 5:22, 23.

What are the works of the flesh?

"Now the works of the flesh are evident, which are: adultery, fornication, uncleanness, lewdness, idolatry, sorcery, hatred, contentions, jealousies, outbursts of wrath, selfish ambitions, dissensions, heresies, envy, murders, drunkenness, revelries, and the like." Verses 19-21.

NOTE—The evils here mentioned are a close parallel to the lists found in Matthew 15:18, 19; Mark 7:20-23; Romans 1:29-31; and 2 Timothy 3:1-5.

How may the works of the flesh be avoided?

"*Walk in the Spirit,* and you shall not fulfill the lust of the flesh." Galatians 5:16.

The Fruit of Love

By what is the love of God shed abroad in the heart?

"The love of God has been poured out in our hearts *by the Holy Spirit* who was given to us." Romans 5:5.

What is love declared to be?

"But above all these things put on love, which is *the bond of perfection.*" Colossians 3:14.

By what does genuine faith work?

"For in Christ Jesus neither circumcision nor uncircumcision avails anything, but *faith working through love.*" Galatians 5:6.

What does love do?

"Hatred stirs up strife, but *love covers all sins.*" Proverbs 10:12. "And above all things have fervent love for one another, for 'love will cover a multitude of sins.'" 1 Peter 4:8.

In what way does love manifest itself?

"Love suffers long and is kind; love does not envy; love does not parade itself, is not puffed up; does not behave rudely, does not seek its own, is not provoked, thinks no evil." 1 Corinthians 13:4, 5.

The Kingdom of God

Of what does the kingdom of God consist?

"For the kingdom of God is not eating and drinking, but *righteousness* and *peace* and *joy* in the Holy Spirit." Romans 14:17.

NOTE—It is the Christian's privilege to have righteousness, peace, and joy—a righteousness which is of God by faith (Romans 3:21, 22); a piece that passeth understanding (Philippians 4:7), which the world can neither give nor take away; and a joy that rejoices evermore (1 Thessalonians 5:16; Philippians 4:4).

Gentleness, Goodness, Faith

What does God's gentleness do for us?

"Your gentleness has *made me great.*" Psalm 18:35.

What spirit should we show toward others?

"And a servant of the Lord must not quarrel but *be gentle to all,* able to teach, patient." 2 Timothy 2:24.

What does the good of God do?

"Or do you despise the riches of His goodness, forbearance, and longsuffering, not knowing that *the goodness of God leads you to repentance?*" Romans 2:4.

How should we treat those who have wronged us?

"Beloved, *do not avenge yourselves,* but rather give place to wrath; for it is written, 'Vengeance is Mine, I will repay,' says the Lord. Therefore *'if your enemy is hungry, feed him; if he is thirsty, give him a drink; for in so doing you will heap coals of fire on his head.'*" Romans 12:19, 20.

How does faith determine our standing with God?

"But *without faith it is impossible to please Him,* for he who comes to God must believe that He is, and that He is a rewarder of those who diligently seek Him." Hebrews 11:6.

Meekness and Self-control

How does God regard the meek and quiet spirit?

"Let your adornment be . . . the hidden person of the heart, with the incorruptible beauty of *a gentle and quiet spirit, which is very precious in the sight of God.*" 1 Peter 3:3, 4.

In our Christian growth and experience, what is to accompany faith, courage, and knowledge?

"But also for this very reason, giving all diligence, add to your faith virtue, to virtue knowledge, to knowledge *self-control.*" 2 Peter 1:5, 6.

NOTE—The word "self-control" means much more than mere abstinence from intoxicating drinks—the limited sense now frequently given to it. It means control, strength, power,

or ascendancy over exciting and evil passions of all kinds. It denotes the self-rule that overcomers or converted individuals have over the evil propensities of their nature. Commenting on this passage, Albert Barnes says: "The influences of the Holy Spirit on the heart make a man moderate in all indulgences; teach him to restrain his passions, and to govern himself."

How are those who control their spirit commanded?

"He who is slow to anger is better than the mighty, and *he who rules his spirit than he who takes a city.*" Proverbs 16:32.

From Condemnation to Peace

What is said of all these different virtues?

"Gentleness, self-control. Against such there is no law." Galatians 5:23.

NOTE—The law condemns sin. But all these things, being virtues, we in harmony with the law. They are produced by the Spirit; and the law, which is spiritual, cannot, therefore, condemn them.

To what unity are Christians exhorted?

"Endeavoring to keep *the unity of the Spirit* in the bond of peace." Ephesians 4:3.

Gifts From the Godhead

Concerning what subject ought we to be informed?

"Now *concerning spiritual gifts,* brethren, I do not want you to be ignorant." 1 Corinthians 12:1.

When Christ ascended, what did He give to humans?

"Therefore He says: 'When He ascended on high, He led captivity captive [literally, "He led captives captive"], and *gave gifts to men.*'" Ephesians 4:8.

What were these gifts that Christ gave?

"And He Himself gave some to be *apostles,* some *prophets,* some *evangelists,* and some *pastors* and *teachers.*" Verse 11.

How are these gifts elsewhere spoken of?

"And God has appointed these in the church: first *apostles,* second *prophets,* third *teachers,* after that *miracles,* then *gifts of healings, helps, administrations, varieties of tongues.*" 1 Corinthians 12:28.

Bible Answers

Purpose of the Gifts

For what purpose were these gifts bestowed upon the church?

"For the equipping of the saints for the work of ministry, for the edifying of the body of Christ . . . ; that we should no longer be children, tossed to and fro and carried about with every wind of doctrine, by the trickery of men, in the cunning craftiness of deceitful plotting, but, speaking the truth in love, may grow up in all things into Him who is the head—Christ." Ephesians 4:12-15.

What result is to be obtained by the exercise of the gifts in the church?

"Till we all come to [literally *"into"*] *the unity of the faith* and of the knowledge of the Son of God, *to a perfect man,* to the measure of the stature of the fullness of Christ." Verse 13.

How is unity preserved in the diversities of gifts?

"There are diversities of gifts, but the *same Spirit."* 1 Corinthians 12:4.

For what purpose is the manifestation of this one Spirit given?

"But the manifestation of the Spirit is given to each one *for the profit of all:* for to one is given the word of wisdom through the Spirit, to another the word of *knowledge* through the same Spirit, to another *faith* by the same Spirit, to another gifts of *healings* by the same Spirit, to another the *working of miracles,* to another *prophecy,* to another *discerning of spirits,* to another *different kinds of tongues,* to another the *interpretation of tongues."* Verses 7-10.

Who controls the distribution of the gifts of the Spirit?

"But one and the *same Spirit* works all these things, distributing to each one individually as He wills." Verse 11.

Was it God's design that all should possess the same gifts?

"Are all apostles? Are all prophets? Are all teachers? Are all workers of miracles? Do all have gifts of healings? Do all speak with tongues? Do all interpret?" Verses 29, 30.

Period of the Gifts

Were the gifts of the Spirit to continue forever?

"Love never fails. But whether there are prophecies, *they will fail;* whether there are tongues, *they will cease;* whether there is knowledge, *it will vanish away."* 1 Corinthians 13:8.

When will the gifts of the Spirit not be needed?

"But *when that which is perfect has come,* then that which is in part will be done away." Verse 10.

Avenues of Communication

How did God communicate with human beings in Eden?

"Then the Lord God *called to Adam and said to him,* 'Where are you?'" Genesis 3:9.

Since the Fall, by what means has God generally made known His will to humans?

"I have also spoken *by the prophets,* and have multiplied visions; I have given symbols *through the witness of the prophets."* Hosea 12:10.

What things belong to God, and what to us?

"The secret things belong to the Lord our God, *but those things which are revealed* belong to us and to our children forever." Deuteronomy 29:29.

How fully and to whom does God reveal His purposes?

"Surely the Lord God does *nothing,* unless *He reveals His secret to His servants the prophets."* Amos 3:7.

The Gift of Prophecy

How does the Lord reveal Himself to His prophets?

"Then He said, 'Hear now My words: if there is a prophet among you, I, the Lord, make Myself known to him in a *vision;* I speak to him in a *dream.'"* Numbers 12:6.

Under what influence did the prophets of old speak?

"For prophecy never came by the will of man, but holy men of God spoke *as they were moved by the Holy Spirit."* 2 Peter 1:21. (See 2 Samuel 23:2.)

How are both the origin of prophecy and the means of communicating it still further shown in God's plan?

"The Revelation of Jesus Christ, which God gave Him to show His servants—things which must shortly take place. And *He sent and signified it by His angel to His servant John."* Revelation 1:1.

What angel revealed to Daniel his visions and dreams?

"Yes, while I was speaking in prayer, the man *Gabriel,* whom I had seen in the vision at the beginning, being caused to fly swiftly, reached me about the time of the evening offering. And *he informed me, and talked with me, and said,* 'O Daniel, I have now come forth to give you skill to understand.'" Daniel 9:21, 22. (See also chapter 10, and Revelation 22:9, 10.)

What Spirit was in the prophets inditing their utterances?

"Of this salvation the prophets have inquired and searched carefully, who prophesied of the grace that would come to you, searching what, or what manner of time, the *Spirit of Christ who was in them* was indicating when He testified beforehand the sufferings of Christ and the glories that would follow." 1 Peter 1:10, 11.

How were the Lord's words to the prophets preserved?

"Daniel had a dream and visions of his head while on his bed. Then *he wrote down the dream,* telling the main facts." Daniel 7:1. (See Jeremiah 51:60; Revelation 1:10, 11.)

By whom has God spoken to us in these last days?

"God, who at various times and in various ways spoke in time past to the fathers by the prophets, has in these last days spoken to us *by His Son.*" Hebrews 1:1, 2.

What was one of the offices to be filled by the Messiah?

"The Lord your God will raise up for you *a Prophet* like me from your midst, from your brethren. Him you shall hear." Deuteronomy 18:15.

Foretelling the Future

Can those who have only the world's wisdom foretell the future?

"Daniel answered in the presence of the king, and said, 'The secret which the king has demanded, the wise men, the astrologers, the magicians, and the soothsayers cannot declare to the king.'" Daniel 2:27.

Who did Daniel say could reveal secrets?

"But *there is a God in heaven who reveals secrets,* and He has made known to King Nebuchadnezzar what will be in the latter days." Verse 28.

How did the prophet Daniel acknowledge the insufficiency of human wisdom?

"*As for me, this secret has not been revealed to me because I have more wisdom than anyone living, but for our sakes* who make known the interpretation to the king, and that you may know the thoughts of your heart." Verse 30.

After revealing and interpreting the dream, what did Daniel say?

"The great God has made known to the king what will come to pass *after this.*" Verse 45.

How does God show His foreknowledge?

"Behold, the former things have come to pass, and *new things I declare; before they spring forth I tell you of them.*" Isaiah 42:9.

What was foretold through the prophet Joel?

"And it shall come to pass afterward that I will pour out My Spirit on all flesh; *your sons and your daughters shall prophesy, your old men shall dream dreams, your young men shall see visions.*" Joel 2:28.

When did this prediction begin to be fulfilled?

"But this is what was spoken by the prophet Joel: 'And it shall come to pass in the last days, says God, that I will pour out of My Spirit on all flesh; your sons and your daughters shall prophesy, your young men shall see visions, your old men shall dream dreams.'" Acts 2:16, 17.

Prophetic Leadership

What were some of the gifts Christ gave to His church?

"'When He ascended on high, He led captivity captive, and gave gifts to men.' . . . And He Himself gave some to be *apostles,* some *prophets,* some *evangelists,* and some *pastors* and *teachers.*" Ephesians 4:8-11.

By what means did God deliver and preserve Israel?

"*By a prophet* the Lord brought Israel out of Egypt, and *by a prophet* he was preserved." Hosea 12:13.

When Moses complained of his slowness of speech, what did God say Aaron should be to him?

"So he shall be your *spokesman* to the people. And he himself shall be as *a mouth* for you, and you shall be to him as God." Exodus 4:16.

What did God afterward call Aaron?

"So the Lord said to Moses: 'See, I have made you as God to Pharaoh, and Aaron . . . shall be *your prophet.*'" Exodus 7:1.

Tests of True and False Prophets

What is one test by which to detect false prophets?

"When a prophet speaks in the name of the Lord, *if the thing does not happen or come to pass,* that is the thing which the Lord has not spoken; the prophet has spoken it presumptuously; you shall not be afraid of him." Deuteronomy 18:22.

What other test should be applied in determining the validity of the claims of a prophet?

Bible Answers

"If there arises among you a prophet or a dreamer of dreams, and he gives you a sign or a wonder, and the sign or the wonder comes to pass, of which he spoke to you, saying, *'Let us go after other gods'*—which you have not known—'and *let us serve them,'* you shall not listen to the words of that prophet or that dreamer of dreams, for the Lord your God is testing you to know whether you love the Lord your God with all your heart and with all your soul. *You shall walk after the Lord your God and fear Him, and keep His commandments and obey His voice;* you shall serve Him and hold fast to Him." Deuteronomy 13:1-4.

NOTE—From these scriptures it will be seen that, in the first place, if a prophet's words do not prove to be true, it is evidence that God has not sent that prophet. On the other hand, even though the thing predicted comes to pass, if the pretended prophet seeks to lead others to break God's commandments, this, regardless of all signs, should be positive evidence that that prophet is not a true one.

What rule did Christ give for distinguishing between true and false prophets?

"Therefore *by their fruits* you will know them." Matthew 7:20.

Attitude Toward God's Prophets

How did God's prophets anciently use the words of former prophets in exhorting the people to obedience?

"Should you not have obeyed the words which the Lord proclaimed through the former prophets when Jerusalem and the cities around it were inhabited and prosperous?" Zechariah 7:7.

What is the promised result of believing God's prophets?

"Believe in the Lord your God, and you shall be established; *believe His prophets, and you shall prosper."* 2 Chronicles 20:20.

What admonition is given regarding the gift of prophecy?

"Do not despise prophecies. Test all things; hold fast what is good." 1 Thessalonians 5:20, 21.

What will characterize the last, or remnant, church?

"And the dragon was enraged with the woman, and he went to make war with the rest of her offspring, *who keep the commandments of God and have the testimony of Jesus Christ."* Revelation 12:17.

What is the "testimony of Jesus"?

"The testimony of Jesus is the spirit of prophecy." Revelation 19:10. (See Revelation 1:9.)

What results when this gift is absent?

"Where there is no revelation, *the people cast off restraint;* but happy is he who keeps the law." Proverbs 29:18. (See also Psalm 74:9.)

Promise and Preparation of Pentecost

For what did Christ, just before His ascension, tell His disciples to wait?

"Behold, I send the Promise of My Father upon you; but tarry in the city of Jerusalem *until you are endued with power from on high."* Luke 24:49.

With what did He say they would be baptized?

"You shall be baptized *with the Holy Spirit* not many days from now." Acts 1:5.

NOTE—John the Baptist had foretold this baptism. He said, "I indeed baptize you with water unto repentance, but He who is coming after me is mightier than I, whose sandals I am not worthy to carry. He will baptize you with the Holy Spirit and fire." Matthew 3:11.

For what work was this baptism to prepare them?

"But you shall receive power when the Holy Spirit has come upon you; and *you shall be witnesses to Me* in Jerusalem, and in all Judea and Samaria, and to the end of the earth." Acts 1:8.

Results of Pentecost

What were some of the results of the preaching of the gospel under the outpouring of the Spirit?

"Now when they heard this, *they were cut to the heart,* and said . . . , 'Men and brethren, what shall we do?' Then Peter said to them, 'Repent, and let every one of you be baptized in the name of Jesus Christ for the remission of sins; and you shall receive the gift of the Holy Spirit. For the promise is to you and to your children, and to all who are afar off, as many as the Lord our God will call.' And with many other words he testified and exhorted them, saying, 'Be saved from this perverse generation.' Then those who gladly received his word were baptized; *and that day about three thousand souls were added to them."* Acts 2:37-41. "And through the hands of the apostles many signs and wonders were done among the people. *And believers were increasingly added to the Lord,* multitudes of both men and women." Acts 5:12-14. "Then the word of God spread, and *the number of the disciples multiplied greatly in Jerusalem,* and a great many of the priests were obedient to the faith." Acts 6:7.

How did persecution affect the preaching of the gospel?

"At that time a great persecution arose against the church which was at Jerusalem; and they were all scattered throughout the regions of Judea and Samaria, except the apostles. . . . Therefore *those who were scattered went everywhere preaching the word.*" Acts 8:1-4.

NOTE—"Persecution has only had a tendency to extend and establish the faith which it was designed to destroy. . . . There is no lesson which men have been so slow to learn as that to oppose and persecute men is the very way to confirm them in their opinions, and to spread their doctrines."—Albert Barnes, on Acts 4:4.

A Latter-Day Outpouring

What prophecy was fulfilled in the Pentecostal outpouring of the Spirit in the time of the apostles?

"But Peter, standing up with the eleven, raised his voice and said to them, ' . . . These are not drunk, as you suppose. . . . But *this is what was spoken by the prophet Joel:* "And it shall come to pass in the last days, says God, that I will pour out of My Spirit on all flesh; your sons and your daughters shall prophesy, your young men shall see visions, your old men shall dream dreams. And on My menservants and on My maidservants I will pour out My Spirit in those days; and they shall prophesy."'" Acts 2:14-18. (See Joel 2:28, 29.)

What expressions in the prophecy of Joel seem to imply a double fulfillment of this outpouring of the Spirit?

"Be glad then, you children of Zion, and rejoice in the Lord your God; for He has given you the *former rain* faithfully, and He will cause the rain to come down for you—the *former rain,* and the *latter rain* in the first month." Joel 2:23. (See also Hosea 6:3.)

NOTE—In Palestine the early rains prepare the soil for the seed sowing, and the latter rains ripen the grain for the harvest. So the early outpouring of the Spirit prepared the world for the extensive sowing of the gospel seed, and the final outpouring will come to ripen the golden grain for the harvest of the earth, which Christ says is "the end of this age." Matthew 13:37-39. (See also Revelation 14:14, 15.)

For what are we told to pray in the time of the "latter rain"?

"*Ask the Lord for rain in the time of the latter rain.* The Lord will make flashing clouds; He will give them showers of rain, grass in the field for everyone." Zechariah 10:1.

NOTE—Before the apostles received the baptism of the Spirit in the early rain on the day of Pentecost, they all "continued with one accord in prayer and supplication." Acts 1:14. During this time they confessed their faults, put away their differences, ceased their selfish ambitions and contentions for place and power, so that when the time for the outpouring came, "they were all with one accord in one place," ready for its reception. To be prepared for the final outpouring of the Spirit, all sin and selfish ambition must again be put away, and a like work of grace wrought upon the hearts of God's people.

The Call of Revelation's Angel

How is the closing gospel work under the outpouring of the Spirit described by the revelator?

"After these things I saw another angel coming down from heaven, having great authority, and *the earth was illuminated with his glory.*" Revelation 18:1.

What does this angel say?

"And he cried mightily with a loud voice, saying, '*Babylon the great is fallen, is fallen,* and has become a dwelling place of demons, a prison for every foul spirit, and a cage for every unclean and hated bird!'" Verse 2.

NOTE—The religious world will then be in much the same condition as was the Jewish nation after it had rejected Christ at His first advent. (See 2 Timothy 3:1-5.)

What did Peter on the day of Pentecost tell his hearers to do?

"And with many other words he testified and exhorted them, saying, '*Be saved from this perverse generation.*'" Acts 2:40.

What similar call and appeal will be made under the final outpouring of the Spirit?

"And I heard another voice from heaven saying, '*Come out of her, my people,* lest you share in her sins, and lest you receive of her plagues. For her sins have reached to heaven, and God has remembered her iniquities.'" Revelation 18:4, 5.

NOTE—A great work will be accomplished in a short time under the final outpouring of the Spirit. Many voices all over the earth will sound the warning cry. Signs and wonders will be wrought by the believers, and as at Pentecost, thousands will be converted in a day.

Those who fail to heed this final gospel call, like the unbelieving Jews, will be doomed to destruction. The seven last plagues will overtake them, as war, famine, death, and destruction overtook the Jews, who, not believing in Christ, failed to heed His call to flee, and shut themselves up in Jerusalem to their doom. Those who heed the call and separate themselves from sin and from sinners will be saved.

The Good News About
Following Christ

What offering did King Hezekiah command to be made when he reestablished the worship of the Temple, following a period of apostasy?

"Then Hezekiah commanded them to offer the *burnt offering* on the altar. And when the burnt offering began, the song of the Lord also began, with the trumpets and with the instruments of David king of Israel." 2 Chronicles 29:27.

How did Hezekiah interpret the meaning of this service to the people of Judah?

"Then Hezekiah answered and said, '*Now that you have consecrated yourselves to the Lord*, come near, and bring sacrifices and thank offerings into the house of the Lord.' So the assembly brought in sacrifices and thank offerings, and as many as were of a willing heart brought burnt offerings." Verse 31.

NOTE—The morning and the evening burnt offering (Exodus 29:38-41) symbolized the daily consecration of the people of the Lord.

Call to Continual Consecration

How does the apostle Paul urge this consecration upon all Christians?

"I beseech you therefore, brethren, by the mercies of God, that you present your bodies a living sacrifice, holy, acceptable to God, which is your reasonable service." Romans 12:1.

What is the sacrifice of praise declared to be?

"Therefore by Him let us continually offer the sacrifice of praise to God, that is, the fruit of our lips, giving thanks to His name." Hebrews 13:15.

How is the service of consecration to be carried forward by the Christian church?

"You also, as living stones, are being built up a spiritual house, a holy priesthood, *to offer up spiritual sacrifices* acceptable to God through Jesus Christ." 1 Peter 2:5.

The Example of Jesus

Who has set the example of complete consecration?

"And whoever desires to be first among you, let him be your slave—just as *the Son of Man* did not come to be served, but to serve, and to give His life a ransom for many." Matthew 20:27, 28.

What position has Jesus taken among His brethren?

"For who is greater, he who sits at the table, or he who serves? Is it not he who sits at the table? Yet *I am among you as the One who serves*." Luke 22:27.

In what does likeness to Christ consist?

"Let this *mind* be in you which was also in Christ Jesus." Philippians 2:5.

What did Christ's spirit of meekness and consecration lead Him to do?

"But made Himself of no reputation, *taking the form of a bondservant,* and coming in the likeness of men." Verse 7.

To what extent did Christ humble Himself?

"And being found in appearance as a man, He humbled Himself and became obedient *to the point of death, even the death of the cross.*" Verse 8.

Call to Complete Consecration

How does He exhort us to the same consecration?

"*Take My yoke upon you and learn from Me,* for I am gentle and lowly in heart, and you will find rest for your souls." Matthew 11:29.

What does He make the condition of discipleship?

"So likewise, whoever of you does not forsake all that he has cannot be My disciple." Luke 14:33.

What is proof that one does not belong to Christ?

"Now if anyone does not have the Spirit of Christ, he is not His." Romans 8:9.

How should one who professes to abide in Christ walk?

"He who says he abides in Him *ought himself also to walk just as He walked.*" 1 John 2:6.

Do we belong to ourselves?

"Do you not know that . . . *you are not your own?* For you were bought at a price." 1 Corinthians 6:19, 20.

What are we therefore exhorted to do?

"For you were bought at a price; therefore *glorify God in your body and in your spirit,* which are God's." Verse 20.

NOTE—Our time, strength, and means are God's, and should be given to His service.

Of what are the bodies of Christians the temple?

"Or do you not know that your body is *the temple of the Holy Spirit* who is in you, whom you have from God?" Verse 19.

For what is one who is truly consecrated ready?

"Also I heard the voice of the Lord, saying: 'Whom shall I send, and who will go for Us?' *Then I said, 'Here am I! Send me.'*" Isaiah 6:8.

How is this willingness for service otherwise expressed?

"Behold, as the eyes of servants look to the hand of their masters, as the eyes of a maid to the hand of her mistress, *so our eyes look to the Lord our God.*" Psalm 123:2.

What Difference Does It Make?

Does it matter what we believe, so long as we are sincere?

"God from the beginning chose you for salvation through sanctification by the Spirit and *belief in the truth.*" 2 Thessalonians 2:13.

NOTE—Doctrine affects the *life.* Truth leads to life and God; error to death and destruction. No one would think of saying it matters not what *god* one worships, so long as they are sincere, any more than they would think of saying it matters not what one *eats* or *drinks,* so long as they *relish* what they eat and drink or what *road* they travel, so long as they *think* they are on the right road. Sincerity is a virtue; but it is not the test of sound doctrine. God wills that we shall know the *truth,* and He has made provision whereby we may *know what is truth.*

Did Joshua think it immaterial what god Israel served?

"Now therefore, fear the Lord, serve Him in sincerity and in truth, and *put away the gods which your fathers served on the other side of the River and in Egypt. Serve the Lord!* And if it seems evil to you to serve the Lord, choose for yourselves this day whom you will serve, whether the gods which your fathers served that were on the other side of the River, or the gods of the Amorites, in whose land you dwell. But as for me and my house, we will serve the Lord." Joshua 24:14, 15.

NOTE—The influence of all idolatrous worship is degrading. (See Romans 1:21-32; Numbers 15; 1 Corinthians 10:20; 1 John 5:21.)

What advice was given to Timothy while he was preparing for the gospel ministry?

"Till I come, give attention to reading, to exhortation, to *doctrine.* . . . Take heed to yourself and to the *doctrine.*" 1 Timothy 4:13-16.

What solemn charge was given him concerning his public work?

"I charge you therefore before God and the Lord Jesus Christ, who will judge the living and the dead at His appearing and His kingdom: *Preach the word!* . . . *Convince, rebuke, exhort, with all longsuffering and teaching.*" 2 Timothy 4:1, 2.

What similar instruction was given to Titus?

"But as for you, speak the things which are proper for *sound doctrine.* . . . In all things [show] yourself to be a pattern of good works; *in doctrine showing integrity,* reverence, incorruptibility." Titus 2:1-7.

Warning Against False Doctrines

Of what kind of doctrines should we beware?

"That we should no longer be children, tossed to and fro and carried about with every *wind of doctrine.*" Ephesians 4:14. (See also Hebrews 13:9.)

What is a "wind of doctrine"?

"And the prophets become *wind,* for *the word is not in them.*" Jeremiah 5:13.

NOTE—Calling a doctrine a wind of doctrine does not make it such. That is a wind of doctrine that is not sustained by the Word of God.

What danger attends the teaching of false doctrine?

"Who have strayed concerning the truth, saying that the resurrection is already past; and they *overthrow the faith of some.*" 2 Timothy 2:18.

Bible Answers

What kind of worship results from false teaching?

"And *in vain they worship Me,* teaching as doctrines the commandments of men." Matthew 15:9.

By what doctrines are some to be misled in the last days?

"Now the Spirit expressly says that in latter times some will depart from the faith, giving heed to deceiving spirits and *doctrines of demons.*" 1 Timothy 4:1. (See 2 Peter 2:1.)

To what would human beings turn their ears?

"For the time will come when they will not endure sound doctrine, but according to their own desires, because they have itching ears, they will heap up for themselves teachers; and they will turn their ears away from the truth, and be turned aside to fables." 2 Timothy 4:3, 4.

The Test of True and False

How may we determine the truthfulness of any doctrine?

"*Test all things;* hold fast what is good." 1 Thessalonians 5:21.

NOTE—The Bible is the test of all doctrine. Whatever does not harmonize and square with this is not to be received. "There is but one standard of the everlastingly right and the everlastingly wrong, and that is the Bible."—T. DeWitt Talmage.

For what is all Scripture profitable?

"All Scripture is given by inspiration of God, and is *profitable for doctrine.*" 2 Timothy 3:16.

What will sound doctrine enable the faithful teacher to do?

"Holding fast the faithful word as he has been taught, that he may be able, *by sound doctrine, both to exhort and convict those who contradict.*" Titus 1:9.

Our Personal Attitude Toward Truth

Who are the disciples of Jesus, and what gracious work does the truth do for those who receive it?

"*If you abide in My word,* you are My disciples indeed. And *you shall know the truth, and the truth shall make you free.*" John 8:31, 32.

Through what are they to be sanctified?

"Sanctify them by *Your truth.* Your word is truth." John 17:17.

Can we close our ears to truth, and remain innocent before God?

"One who turns away his ear from hearing the law, even *his prayer is an abomination.*" Proverbs 28:9.

What did Christ say of those who will to do God's will?

"If anyone wills to do His will, *he shall know concerning the doctrine,* whether it is from God or whether I speak on My own authority." John 7:17. (See also Psalm 25:9; John 8:12.)

Results of Our Choice

What will God allow to come to those who reject truth?

"Because they did not receive the love of the truth, that they might be saved. And for this reason God will send them *strong delusion,* that they should believe the lie, that they all may be condemned who did not believe the truth but had pleasure in unrighteousness." 2 Thessalonians 2:10-12.

What fate awaits blind teachers and their followers?

"Let them alone. They are blind leaders of the blind. And if the blind leads the blind, *both will fall into a ditch.*" Matthew 15:14.

To whom will the gates of the heavenly city finally be opened?

"Open the gates, that the righteous nation which keeps the truth may enter in." Isaiah 26:2. (See also Revelation 22:14.)

Walking in the Light

How important is it that we walk in the light when it comes to us?

"Walk while you have the light, *lest darkness overtake you;* he who walks in darkness does not know where he is going." John 12:35.

NOTE—It is important to settle a plain question of duty at once, and not delay obedience under the excuse of waiting for more light. To do as did Balaam—ask God again concerning that which He has plainly and expressly spoken—is dangerous. Nor should we, like the unbelieving Jews, seek a sign from Heaven to convince us that we ought to obey the Written Word. Has God spoken? Is it His word? Then obey. Do not insult Heaven with the question whether it is right to obey. (See 1 Kings 22:1-36; Ezekiel 14:1-5.)

Upon what condition are we promised cleansing from sin?

"But if we walk in the light as He is in the light, we have

fellowship with one another, and the blood of Jesus Christ His Son cleanses us from all sin." 1 John 1:7.

Sources of Light

Who is the light of the world?

"*I am the light of the world.* He who follows Me shall not walk in darkness, but have the light of life." John 8:12.

How are we to walk in Christ?

"*As you therefore have received Christ Jesus the Lord,* so walk in Him." Colossians 2:6.

What has God given to guide our feet aright in the path of truth and duty?

"*Your word is a lamp* to my feet and a *light* to my path." Psalm 119:105. (See Proverbs 6:23.)

What does the entrance of God's Word give?

"The entrance of Your words *gives light;* it gives understanding to the simple." Psalm 119:130.

Who does Christ say will be blessed through the prophecies of the book of Revelation?

"Blessed is *he who reads* and *those who hear* the words of this prophecy, *and keep those things which are written in it.*" Revelation 1:3.

NOTE—We are in the last days, in the generation that is to hear the final warning message contained in this book. (See Revelation 14:6-10; 18:1-5.)

More Light for the Righteous

How long may the just expect increased light to shine upon their pathway?

"But the path of the just is like the shining sun, *that shines ever brighter unto the perfect day.*" Proverbs 4:18.

NOTE—The more earnestly one desires to know the will of God, while living up to all the light they have, the more light and truth from God will shine upon their pathway. If light is sown for the righteous, such are the very ones who may expect advanced light to come to them, and to see new duties presented to them from a study of the Word of God.

How did God respond to Cornelius' sincerity of worship?

"He saw clearly in a vision *an angel of God coming in and saying to him, 'Cornelius!'* And when he observed him, he was afraid, and said, 'What is it, lord?' So he said to him, 'Your prayers and your alms have come up for a memorial before God.'" Acts 10:3, 4.

Because Cornelius' ways pleased the Lord, was this evidence that he had nothing more to learn or do?

"Now send men to Joppa, and send for Simon whose surname is Peter. He is lodging with Simon, a tanner, whose house is by the sea. *He will tell you what you must do.*" Verses 5, 6.

NOTE—The Lord favored Cornelius with a visit from one of His angels not because Cornelius knew the way of salvation perfectly, but because the Lord saw in him a sincere desire for more light and willing mind to comply with every known requirement. That spirit was pleasing to God. All may now receive advanced light if, like Cornelius, they seek it and are willing to walk in it when it comes to them. If it is neglected, they are guilty before God and will be left to the buffetings of the enemy.

Results of Our Choice

What will become of the light that one has but fails to walk in it?

"The lamp of the body is the eye. Therefore, when your eye is good, your whole body also is full of light. But when your eye is bad, your body also is full of darkness. Therefore *take heed that the light which is in you is not darkness.*" Luke 11:34, 35.

Why are those condemned that do not come to the light?

"And this is the condemnation, that the light has come into the world, and *men loved darkness rather than light, because their deeds were evil.*" John 3:19.

What will one who is really seeking for truth do?

"But he who does the truth *comes to the light,* that his deeds may be clearly seen, that they have been done in God." Verse 21.

What will those who reject light and truth finally be led to believe?

"And for this reason God will send them strong delusion, *that they should believe the lie,* that they all may be condemned who did not believe the truth but had pleasure in unrighteousness." 2 Thessalonians 2:11, 12.

NOTE—The opposite of light is darkness; the opposite of truth is a lie. For those who reject light and truth, only darkness and error remain. God is sometimes in the Scriptures represented as sending that which He permits to come.

Upon what condition only may we be made partakers of Christ?

"For we have become partakers of Christ *if we hold the beginning of our confidence steadfast to the end.*" Hebrews 3:14.

Index

Abraham 20
Alcohol 94, 95
Angels 36, 70, 103
Atonement, day of 71, 72

Babylon 5, 6, 83, 84, 95
Baptism 54, 56, 102
Beast in prophecy 83-86
Bible, Christ in 7
    origin of 7
    power of 8
Birth, new 29
Blood, sacrificial 71-73

Charity 75
Charlemagne 6
Charles V 6
Choice, results of 106, 108
Christ, baptism of 56
    birth of, foretold 11
    incarnation of 18
    preexistence of 17
    prophecies of 17, 35
    resurrection of 11, 54, 56
    return of 11, 36, 78, 79
Christ and the Sabbath 44-46
Church, true 81
City, Holy 22, 23
Clay 5, 6
Comforter 96-103
Commandments, Ten 53, 71
Confession 26
Consecration 104
Conversion 29
Covetousness 91
Creation 8, 9, 19, 40, 57, 74
    new 29

Daniel 5, 32, 67, 68, 73, 94, 95, 101
Death 38, 53, 57
    second 63
Devil 20, 81
Diet 92, 94, 95
Discipleship 104
Disease 92
Doctrines, false 105, 106
Dragon 81, 84, 86, 87
Dreams 5
Drunkards 95

Earth, new 20, 22, 63
Earthquakes 31
Eternal life 23
Eunuch 56

Faith 24, 52, 79, 99
Faithfulness 76, 77
Famine 31
Fire 62, 63
Flood 15
Food principles 92
Forgiveness 26, 28

Gabriel 67, 68
God, character of 8, 12
    characteristics of 12
    kingdom of 97, 99
    love of 12, 13
    nature of 12
Gospel 52, 53
Grace 53, 75
Greece 6

Health 92, 94
Hell 62, 63
Hitler 6
Holy Spirit 56, 68, 96-103
    fruit of 97
Humanity, nature of 57

Immortality 19, 59

Jerusalem 31, 45, 69
    New 22, 23
Judgment 67-74
    investigative 70
Justification 53

Laodicea, Council of 49
Latter rain 104
Law 52, 53
Life, eternal 19, 58
    in Christ 23
Lord's Day 46, 47
Love, fruit of 97

Manna 41
Medes 6
Meditation 78
Meekness 99
Millennium 64-66

Napoleon 6
Nature, divine 75
Nebuchadnezzar 5
New birth 29

Offering 91

Pardon 26
Patience 75, 79
Peace 99
Pentecost 96, 102, 103
Persecution 82, 102, 103
Perseverance 75, 79
Persians 6
Pestilences 31
Prayer 77-80
Prodigal son 26, 28
Prophets, false 101, 102
Prophecy 31
    gift of 100, 101
Protestants 51

Redemption 8
Remnant church 76
Repentance 25, 54
Resurrection, of saints 60, 61, 64
    of wicked 64-66
Rome 6, 83-85

Sabbath 40, 74
    change of 48-51
Sabbathkeeping 44
Salvation 25, 26, 37, 59, 74
Sanctuary 70-73
    heavenly 70, 71
Satan 19, 20, 36, 76, 81, 84
Second Coming, signs of 32, 33, 35
Self-control 75, 94, 95, 99
Sin, end of 14-16
    origin of 14
Sleep 59, 60
Soul 57, 58, 62
Spirit, Holy 56, 68, 96-103
    human 58
Spiritual gifts 99-101
Suffering, origin of 14
Sunday 49-51, 87-89

Temperance 75, 94, 95, 99

Temple 31
Thanksgiving 78
Thousand years 64-66
Tithe 90
Truth 106
Twenty-three hundred days 67-70

United States 85, 86

Victory 76, 77
Vision 5, 73

Warfare, Christian 76
Wars 31, 65
Wilhelm, Kaiser 6
Women in prophecy 81

More Family Reading

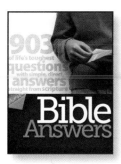

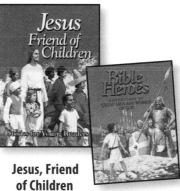

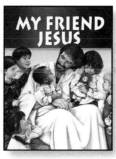

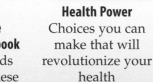

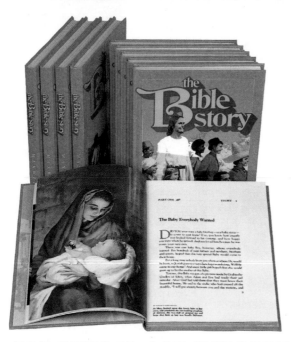

FOR SCHOOL-AGE CHILDREN

The Bible Story

This is the most accurate and complete set of children's Bible story books available. More than 400 Bible stories are included, with full-color paintings at every page opening. Unlike television, these stories introduce children to heroes you would be proud to have them imitate. These stories are also an excellent tool for loving parents who want their children to grow up making right decisions and making them with confidence. Ten volumes, hardcover.

Uncle Arthur's Bedtime Stories

For years this collection of stories has been the center of cozy reading experiences between parents and children. Arthur Maxwell tells the real-life adventures of young children—adventures that teach the importance of such character traits as kindness and honesty. Discover how a hollow pie taught Robert not to be greedy and how an apple pie shared by Annie saved her life. Five volumes, hardcover.

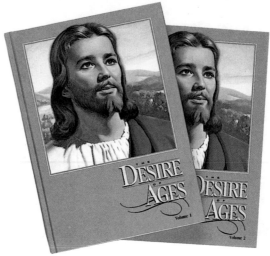

The Desire of Ages

This is E. G. White's monumental best seller on the life of Christ. It is perhaps the most spiritually perceptive of the Savior's biographies since the Gospel According to John. Here Jesus becomes more than a historic figure—He is the great divine-human personality set forth in a hostile world to make peace between God and humanity. Two volumes, hardcover.

FOR PRESCHOOL CHILDREN

My Bible Friends

Imagine your child's delight as you read the charming story of Small Donkey, who carried tired Mary up the hill toward Bethlehem. Or of Zacchaeus the Cheater, who climbed a sycamore tree so he could see Jesus passing by. Each book has four attention-holding stories written in simple, crystal-clear language. And the colorful illustrations surpass in quality what you may have seen in any other children's Bible story book. Five volumes, hardcover. Also available in videos and audiocassettes.

FOR MORE INFORMATION, write: *The Bible Story*, P.O. Box 1119, Hagerstown, MD 21741.